The Elderly and Old Age Support
in Rural China

The Elderly and Old Age Support in Rural China

Challenges and Prospects

Fang Cai, John Giles, Philip O'Keefe and Dewen Wang

THE WORLD BANK
Washington, D.C.

ISBN: 978-0-8213-8685-9
eISBN: 978-0-8213-8903-4
DOI: 10.1596/978-0-8213-8685-9

Cover design: Naylor Design, Inc.
Cover photo: iStockphoto.com

Library of Congress Cataloging-in-Publication Data has been requested

Contents

Tables

Foreword

Many countries face policy challenges related to the well-being of their aging populations, and China is no different. What distinguishes it is that rapid population aging is occurring in society at a significantly lower income level than in members of the Organisation for Economic Co-operation and Development or, more recently, East Asian countries. Although the broad direction and scale of the aging transition in China have been known for some time, less work has been done to understand the household-level effects and implications for public policy. This book looks at the well-being of rural elderly people, a substantial and growing share of China's elderly population and one that faces particular problems. It first provides detailed empirical analysis of the welfare and living conditions of the rural elderly since the early 1990s in the context of large-scale rural-to-urban migration. It then goes on to explore the evolution of the rural pension system in China over the past two decades and to raise issues on that system's current implementation and future directions.

Several findings emerge that have implications well beyond pension policy. First, aging is going to be faster in rural than urban areas, with the rural old-age dependency ratio rising by more than two and a half times by 2030 and the gap with urban areas widening. The book also shows that rural elderly people have, to date, been significantly worse off, relative both to urban elderly people and to younger rural people. This finding occurs even though the rural elderly have longer working lives and save a substantial share of income across their life cycle. Rural elderly people remain much more dependent on their own labor and on support from their families than the urban elderly, who have historically had higher access to government pensions.

The mass rural-to-urban migration that has happened in China since the 1990s is changing the context of family support to rural elderly people. This change can be seen in the rapid shift in living arrangements in rural areas, where co-residence of rural elderly with their adult children fell from 70 percent in 1991 to 40 percent by 2006. The book documents the complex dynamics of migration and household behavior, with positive effects on elderly rural incomes from migrant remittances, but also sometimes burdensome obligations for the rural elderly to continue working the land into old age and to care for their "left behind" grandchildren.

The Chinese authorities have initiated policies that seek to strengthen public support to rural elderly households. A national Rural Pension Pilot Scheme was introduced in late 2009 and has been rapidly expanded subsequently, with full geographic coverage planned by end-2012. A national rural social assistance program (*dibao*) was rolled out in 2007 and now covers close to 50 million people, many of them from poor rural elderly households. The New Cooperative Medical Scheme of health insurance has been rapidly expanded, achieving around 95 percent coverage. It has been of particular value for older people in rural areas.

The book is a collaborative effort between the Institute of Population and Labor Economics of the Chinese Academy of Social Sciences and the World Bank. It has benefited from insights from officials in the Ministry of Human Resources and Social Security and the Ministry of Finance, as well as from those of colleagues at the World Bank. The Bank hopes the book will not only contribute to deepening the understanding of demographic change in rural China but also highlight the substantial knowledge gaps that remain. How the country manages the aging of its population will be one of the major challenges it faces in coming decades, the success of which will have implications for not only China but also the whole world.

Klaus Rohland
Country Director for China
World Bank, Beijing

Acknowledgments

This book is based primarily on two background studies that were produced as part of a collaboration with the Chinese Academy of Social Sciences (CASS) Institute for Population and Labor Economics. The first study, titled "The Well-Being of China's Rural Elderly," is by Fang Cai (CASS), John Giles of the World Bank's Development Economics Research Group (DECRG), and Dewen Wang of the East Asia Human Development Sector Social Protection Unit (EASHS). It is the basis for chapters 1–4. The second study is by Yuning Wu from the Chinese Academy of Labor and Social Security (CALSS) and it informed chapter 5. In addition, chapters 5 and 6 drew upon work of Philip O'Keefe for the World Bank China Pensions Framework Paper (World Bank forthcoming). The study was initiated by Xiaoqing Yu of the Human Development Unit in the East Asia and Pacific Region of the World Bank (EASHD) and was subsequently comanaged by Philip O'Keefe (EASHD) and John Giles (DECRG). Lansong Zhang and Limei Sun also assisted in finalizing the draft. The study benefited from internal review within the World Bank and, in particular, peer review by Robert Palacios (South Asia Human Development Department) and John Blomquist (Middle East and North Africa Human Development

Department). The sector director who guided preparation was Emmanuel Jimenez (EASHD). The team also benefited from useful discussions with Ardo Hansson (EASPR), Mark Dorfman (Human Development Network Social Protection and task manager of the China Pensions Framework Paper), Robert Holzmann (special adviser), and Yvonne Sin (Tower Watson).

Contributors

Fang Cai is professor and director of the Center for Population and Labor Economics at the Chinese Academy of Social Sciences. A leading and influential economist and demographer in China, Professor Cai coauthored the influential books *The China Miracle: Development Strategy and Economic Reform* (2003) with Justin Lin and Zhou Li and *The Chinese Economy: Reform and Development* (2009) with Justin Lin and Yong Cao.

John Giles is senior labor economist in the Development Research Group at the World Bank. His current research interests include the movement of labor from agricultural to nonagricultural employment, internal migration and its effects on households and communities, poverty traps, household risk-coping and risk-management behavior, population aging and retirement decisions in developing countries, and the relationship between social protection systems and labor supply decisions. Prior to joining the World Bank in 2007, he was associate professor of economics at Michigan State University.

Philip O'Keefe is lead economist and Human Development Sector coordinator for China and Mongolia in the East Asia and Pacific Region of the World Bank. He has worked on social protection, labor market, and social services in Eastern Europe and Central Asia, India and Nepal, and the Pacific Islands. Prior to joining the World Bank in 1993, he was university lecturer in International Economic Law at the University of Warwick, U.K.

Dewen Wang is social protection economist in the World Bank's Beijing Office. His work focuses on China's social insurance and social assistance programs, labor market dynamics, demographic transition, and population aging. He was professor and division chief of the Institute of Population and Labor Economics, Chinese Academy of Social Sciences, before he joined the Word Bank Social Protection team.

Abbreviations

ADL	activity of daily living
CASS	China Academy of Social Sciences
CHNS	China Health and Nutrition Survey
CPC	Communist Party of China
CURES	China Urban and Rural Elderly Survey
GDP	gross domestic product
IPLE	Institute of Population and Labor Economics
MDC	matching defined contribution
MHRSS	Ministry of Human Resources and Social Security
MOA	Ministry of Agriculture
MOCA	Ministry of Civil Affairs
MOLSS	Ministry of Labor and Social Security
NBS	National Bureau of Statistics
NDC	notional defined contribution
NSSF	National Social Security Fund
OECD	Organisation for Economic Co-operation and Development
RCRE	Research Center for Rural Economy
RMB	renminbi
TFR	total fertility rate
US$	U.S. dollar

Executive Summary

Although average incomes in China have risen dramatically since the 1980s, concerns are increasing that the rural elderly have not benefited from growth to the same extent as younger people and the urban elderly. Concerns about welfare of the rural elderly combine spatial and demographic issues. Large gaps exist between conditions in coastal and interior regions and between conditions in urban and rural areas of the country. In addition to differences in income by geography, considerable differences exist across demographic groups in the level of coverage by safety nets, in the benefits received through the social welfare system, and in the risks of falling into poverty. In particular, older residents of rural China may be more likely to be left behind than younger cohorts and their urban elderly peers because of lack of pension support, insufficient savings, and migration of adult children. The China poverty assessment estimated that the elderly made up 8.5 percent of China's poor in 2003, and that 12.8 and 13.0 percent of elderly men and women, respectively, lived in poverty (Chaudhuri and Datt 2009). It did not, however, examine separately the poverty status of rural and urban elderly, nor did it look in detail at the sources of support, saving behavior, and other issues associated with the elderly population, particularly the rural elderly.

This book aims to do two things: first, it provides detailed empirical analysis of the welfare and living conditions of the rural elderly since the early 1990s in the context of large-scale rural-to-urban migration, and second, it explores the evolution of the rural pension system in China over the past two decades and raises a number of issues on its current implementation and future directions. Although the two sections of the book are distinct in analytical terms, they are closely linked in policy terms: the first section demonstrates in several ways a rationale for greater public intervention in the welfare of the rural elderly, and the second documents the response of policy to date and options to consider for deepening the coverage and effects of the rural pension system over the longer term.

The section on welfare of the rural elderly (chapters 1–4) attempts to answer several questions that are relevant to understanding the rationale for public support for the rural elderly.[1] First, it examines demographic trends to establish the extent of aging and old-age dependency over time in China. It then explores the incidence of poverty and vulnerability among the rural elderly, both over time and relative to other groups of the population. After finding cause for significant concern related to rural elderly poverty and vulnerability, it then looks at the evolution of sources of support for the rural elderly to assess their relative importance and effects on household incomes. Given their importance, own-labor income and support from family are treated in more detail. Finally, the first section looks at saving behavior among both the working-age and elderly populations, across the income distribution and over time. The key findings with respect to rural elderly welfare are as follows:

- *Demographic projections for rural China made for this book and based on various fertility and migration scenarios suggest that the demographic transition is accelerating and that aging is far more pronounced in rural than in urban areas* (see chapter 1). In 2008, rural and urban old-age dependency ratios were 13.5 percent and 9.0 percent, respectively—a gap of 4.5 percentage points. The gap in old-age dependency ratios will widen to 13.3 percentage points by 2030 when the old-age dependency ratio will reach 34.4 percent in rural areas and 21.1 percent in urban areas. With the demographic transition and continued movement of young adults into cities, families will be subject to further strain to support future generations of the rural elderly.

- *The rural elderly have been consistently poorer and more vulnerable than both working-age households and the urban elderly in China over time, and this finding includes the incidence of chronic poverty* (see chapter 2). In addition to higher poverty rates, households headed by the rural elderly have been more vulnerable to poverty since the early 1990s, and the declines in vulnerability caused by economic growth have been less pronounced than for working-age households. The rural elderly 71–80 years of age have the highest poverty rates (with a correspondingly slower reduction in poverty rates between the 1990s and mid-2000s), while those over 80 have lower poverty rates than the working-age population as they increasingly coreside with their adult children. Although location has played a reduced role as a determinant of poverty in rural elderly households over time (as for all rural households), location remains a stronger determinant of the welfare of rural elderly households than of other rural households. In terms of the factors that affect the incomes of the rural elderly, some (such as obtaining higher education levels and having a pension) are positive, as expected. The effect of having a migrant child is, however, more complex. Although having a migrant child per se has an inconclusive impact on the income of elderly rural households, having migrant children has a clearer and positive impact in terms of ability to cope with shocks to household income, whether communitywide or household specific. As a result, households with migrant children are 26 percent less likely to have incomes below the poverty line and are far less likely to become poor because of health shocks.

- *Sources of support for the rural elderly differ significantly from those of the urban elderly and also change sharply among the rural elderly during their sixties* (see chapter 3). The rural elderly depend far more on their own labor and family support than the urban elderly (for whom pensions also play a critical role), and family support becomes more important as older rural populations age. This finding is true even though coresidence of rural elderly with adult children has fallen from 70 percent in 1991 to 40 percent by 2006. The rural elderly work as long as they can, but even then remain very dependent on family support. To understand both the adequacy of this support for rural elderly welfare and its likely responsiveness to public subsidies for old-age support, the book examines the responsiveness of private transfers by family members to low-income households headed by elderly residents. It finds little evidence that public transfers would crowd out private transfers, even at very low levels of income per capita. In addition, the ability of adult children to provide private transfers may be subject to considerable uncertainty. The children of the rural elderly are frequently employed as informal sector workers in nonagricultural activities either locally or in migrant destinations. Given that adult children's own incomes are risky, examining the variance in expected private transfers is important, because some variance in adult child income is likely passed on to parents. The book finds that low-income rural elderly face the risk that transfers from adult children may not be sufficient to keep them out of poverty.

- *A considerable share of the rural elderly work well beyond age 70, though labor as the primary source of support falls sharply during their sixties.* This finding is consistent with research on elderly labor supply, which provides evidence that China's rural elderly continue to work well beyond age 60 out of necessity and only stop working when physically incapacitated. The book also examines the effects of both adult child migration and increasing family wealth on labor-supply decisions of the elderly. As would be expected, rural elderly in wealthier households are less likely to be working, as are those with more educated household members and pensions. However, the effect of a migrant worker in itself is less clear, possibly because of the offsetting effects of higher income from remittances (which decrease the chances of work by the rural elderly) and the need to keep family land in use to retain it (which creates incentives for elderly family members who stay in rural locations to keep working the land).

- *Saving patterns across the age distribution in China are high and remain positive even in old age, despite falling after 55 years of age. However, savings are strongly correlated with household income, and the rural poor are not saving on average* (see chapter 4). The book finds that households without elderly members have higher saving rates, though the gap is narrowing, and those with migrant members have higher saving rates than those without (including households with elderly members). As might be expected, saving rates decline with age after age 55, but the average saving rate always remains positive, even into advanced old age. Little comparable decline occurs in saving rates in elderly households with migrants, which likely reflects the perceived transitory nature of remittance income. The difference in saving behaviors between rural households with and without social security benefits is significant and consistent over time, which is further verified when findings are broken down by income quintile group.

The analysis in chapters 1–4 provides the rationale for public sector intervention in rural old-age welfare, and the Chinese authorities are committed to rapidly expanding coverage of the rural pension under the national pilot scheme launched in 2009. Given the directions of national policy, the second section of the book (chapters 5 and 6) looks at China's experience with pensions for the rural elderly and the lessons of experience since the 1990s, including observations on the initial implementation of the national rural pension pilot. Chapter 6 discusses key issues for the rural pension system in the longer term, and raises a number of options for consideration in the evolution of the system that may help it achieve the government's policy objectives even more effectively over time. It also reviews relevant international experience in both matching defined contribution schemes and social pensions.

The experience with rural pensions in China during the 1990s and 2000s has been piecemeal but provides a number of important lessons that have informed design of the new national scheme. Prior experience with rural pensions (including the wave of local pilots since the early 2000s) suggests that several issues need close attention in the funded portion of the rural pension system, including the following: (a) the regulation and oversight of funded portions of rural pensions, which have been—and in many areas remain—significantly underdeveloped; (b) the need for a public subsidy to incentivize sustained participation of rural workers, and issues of the balance of public subsidy among levels of government, the individual, and the collective economy; (c) the relatively low retirement ages (often 60 or below) that are understandable given the current ages in the urban system and have been retained in the national pilot, but will be important to raise to reflect the rapidly changing demographics of rural areas; (d) the interaction of pension benefits with the consolidating rural social assistance system to ensure policy coherence across the social protection system; (e) the challenges of the portfolio investment rules on funded pensions leading to very low rates of return; (f) the very localized management of pension accumulations, presenting challenges of weak local capacity and failure to exploit economies of scale; and (g) the portability rules and implementing mechanisms between the rural pension system and the urban systems.

The national pension pilot is an exciting and positive development in terms of expanding pension coverage to the rural population. Moreover, some adaptations of the national rural pension pilot have the potential to increase the strengths of the system over time. Chapter 6 gives options that the government could consider as it expands the current schemes for rural workers (and parallel schemes for urban residents) over time. The chapter also lays out relevant international experience.[2] The following key issues are addressed:

- *Inclusion of a matching defined contribution element in the national pilot and the appropriate level of the matching subsidy and its functions relative to the basic pension benefit in terms of incentives to participate in the scheme.* Although a single "correct" level of matching subsidy is difficult to define, emerging international experience suggests that considering a stronger role for the matching subsidy as the system evolves could have merit.

- *Rules for investment and management of individual account contributions, and options for reducing the challenges of low rates of return that have been seen in the urban funded system.* The chapter makes a number of suggestions for consideration as the system evolves. The first is the desirability of some guaranteed rate of return on individual account accumulations, preferably national gross domestic product. The second is that the introduction of a reserve fund to address fluctuations in returns on individual accounts or the exhaustion of benefits caused by longevity may be worth considering. Third, the authorities might consider using age-based portfolio default rules that provide for more aggressive investment for younger contributors that gradually becomes more conservative over the life cycle to focus on preserving the value of accumulations at retirement. A fourth issue is whether in the medium term permitting account holders to borrow a portion of their account accumulations at a specified interest rate and with legally binding repayment conditions is desirable for the individual account. Finally, the management of funds in individual accounts and the appropriate level of the system for doing this merit consideration. Current pilot schemes and past practice have generally involved management at the county level. However, clear benefits exist to combining funds from localities into a single pot of money that can be managed at higher levels to generate economies of scale in fund management. Previous experience with rural pensions in China cautions against localized management and investment of accumulations.

- *Whether the basic pension benefit in the national pilot should in time evolve into a "social pension" in which coverage is not dependent on contributions.* International experience reviewed later in this section suggests that achieving full pension coverage is very difficult at the level of the individual in rural and informal sector schemes based on approaches that require contributions, even when incentives are provided to contribute. A social pension approach—as used in all countries of the Organisation for Economic Co-operation and Development and in a growing number of developing countries—would be broadly consistent with the design of the basic benefit provision under the rural pension pilot, and this book believes it is worthy of serious consideration as the rural pension system evolves (as well as having potential relevance for emerging "urban resident" schemes). Any social pension should be subjected to a pension test that would adjust the amount paid to those ages 65 to 74 by a proportion of benefits they receive either from an individual account or from an urban workers' pension.

- *Transition and portability issues.* These will become important as the national rural pension scheme matures. The first type of transition is from old to new rural pension schemes within the same locality. Practice in China has varied, with areas such as Beijing allowing portability of funded accumulations from old to new schemes, whereas other areas, such as the province of Hunan, stipulate that participants must close out their accounts in old schemes before starting afresh in new pilots. The national scheme appears to allow transfers of balances from prior schemes. The second (and ultimately more important) issue is portability between rural and urban schemes (or migrant-worker schemes located in urban areas where these exist). This issue will be critical to reaching the government's stated goal of an integrated social security system by 2020. The ease with which this transfer can be done has varied according to scheme design and the compatibility of rural pilots with existing urban schemes. In principle, in all schemes, the funded portion is easily made portable. Because the matching defined contribution design adopted in the national rural pilot has no social pooling, no issues of apportionment arise.

The issue of portability raises a host of design and implementation questions that will need to be closely considered during the pilot phase of the rural pension pilot. When a worker moves, will the funds in his or her account move, or will only his or her contribution records do so? How will the system account for accumulations in the rural system when workers move to the urban system? Finally, are pensions paid from various locations or from a single payment authority? These questions raise issues for record keeping, communication and information exchange between systems, and the exchange of account information. In principle, such questions should be capable of being addressed by standardized record-keeping and reporting formats for the new rural pension system being disseminated by the Ministry of Human Resources and Social Security. Harmonization of fund transfer and pension disbursement procedures would also be required. Again, some degree of centralization would be desirable to lessen administrative demands at the lower levels, although this might be at the provincial level within national guidelines. Elaborated guidance from the central authorities on these issues will be necessary over time.

- *Interaction between the funded portion of the rural pension system and the basic benefit in the longer term.* A key policy decision relates to whether individual accounts and the basic benefit (or social pension) should be combined over time as the contributory system matures. The two broad options are (a) to retain a basic benefit/social pension for persons over a certain age to provide an income floor that is supplemented by benefits from individual accounts, or (b) to gradually phase out the basic benefit/social pension as the contributory system matures, addressing elderly poverty through the regular social assistance program (perhaps, as is the case in a number of urban areas already, with an elderly supplement on the *dibao* threshold or benefit level). This book recommends that the basic benefit/social pension should be retained even in the longer run and cites the case of Chile as an instructive model of the interaction of social pensions and individual accounts that strikes a sensible balance between poverty and incentive concerns.

- *Future integration between urban and rural pension systems and the issue of portability.* Although "integration" is unlikely in the foreseeable future to imply full equalization of benefits between rural and urban areas, a common design framework would be useful to facilitate portability between systems. This can already be seen in several areas, where integrated pension schemes for rural and urban residents are in place (for example, Zhongshan in Guangdong Province).

Notes

1. The first section is drawn from the background paper by Cai, Giles, and Wang (2009), which uses a rich variety of data sources to examine various dimensions of rural elderly welfare.
2. This chapter is an adapted and shortened form of the annex on rural pensions in the forthcoming Pensions Framework Paper (World Bank forthcoming). That paper covers all elements of the Chinese pension system in a more comprehensive manner, and consultations on the draft were carried out in 2010.

References

Cai, Fang, John Giles, and DewenWang. 2009. "The Well-Being of China's Rural Elderly." Background Paper for East Asia Social Protection Team, World Bank, Washington, DC.

Chaudhuri, Shubham and Gausav Datt. 2009. *From Poor Areas to Poor People: China's Evolving Poverty Agenda, An Assessment of Poverty and Inequality in China*. Washington, DC: World Bank.

World Bank. Forthcoming. *China: A Vision for Pension Policy Reform Options*. Washington, DC: World Bank.

CHAPTER 1

Trends in the Aging of China's Rural Population: Past, Present, and Future

China's rapid demographic transition has led to the shrinking of the working-age share of the population and has raised concerns about population aging. Concerns have arisen over the old-age support and social security system in both rural and urban areas, as have worries about potential labor supply and labor market shortages in the future and the appropriateness of fertility and family-planning policies. This chapter reviews China's demographic transition, with a particular focus on rural areas and on aging and fertility. Results are based on new estimates from a team comprising the China Academy of Social Sciences (CASS), China's National Bureau of Statistics (NBS), and the World Bank. These estimates emphasize the importance of understanding the effects of migration on population structure and distribution. Not only will old-age dependency ratios rise rapidly, but this trend is likely to be much more pronounced in rural areas (consistent with anecdotal concerns about the "hollowing out" of villages because of migration). Such changes are likely to put additional strains on informal support networks, which are already unable to provide full support to their elderly members.[1]

Demographic Transition in China

In the planned-economy period, fertility was high in most years, except for the period between 1958 and 1961. As shown in figure 1.1, the average birthrate was more than 3.06 percent during the prereform period but witnessed a sharp decline after the mid-1970s with implementation of China's family planning policy. The death rate had dropped earlier to below 1.00 percent after the introduction of a rural cooperative medical system in the early 1960s and has held at roughly 0.65 percent since the beginning of the reform period. A declining birthrate with a low and stable death rate is a feature of China's low-fertility era.

From 1978 to 2008, China's annual population growth rate dropped from 1.20 to 0.51 percent. The tremendous decline can be attributed to two sources: the implementation of family planning policies and the effect of economic reforms (Gu and others 2007; Johnson 1994; Schultz and Yi 1999; Vermeer 2006). One-child policies were first implemented in cities and then extended to the countryside, leading to an abrupt decline in total fertility during the late 1970s. As figure 1.2 shows, the sharp drop contrasts with changes in fertility in other developing countries during the 1970s. Since 1990, China's total fertility rate (TFR) has approached that of developed countries. Another important factor in recent years has been rural-to-urban migration. Increasing nonagricultural employment opportunities have caused rural migrants to postpone marriage and thus delay fertility.

Over the past 40 years, China has experienced the demographic transition to an "aging society" that typically took more than 100 years in such developed countries as the United Kingdom, the United States, and the Nordic countries (Uhlenberg 2009). Similarly, most of these developed countries had rural pension systems in place long before populations started to age (see box 1.1). By international standards, a society is said to be aging when (a) more than 10 percent of the population is over 60 years of age, and (b) more than 7 percent is over 65. As shown in figure 1.3, China entered the ranks of aging societies in 2000, when the over-60 and over-65 shares of the population reached 10.5 percent and 7.0 percent, respectively.

Population aging has been uneven between rural and urban areas during China's demographic transition, with rural areas aging more rapidly. Even though fertility is higher in rural areas than in urban areas, the elderly proportion of the rural population is also higher. As shown in figure 1.4, the gap of aged population between rural and urban areas has

Figure 1.1   Population Growth in China, 1949–2008

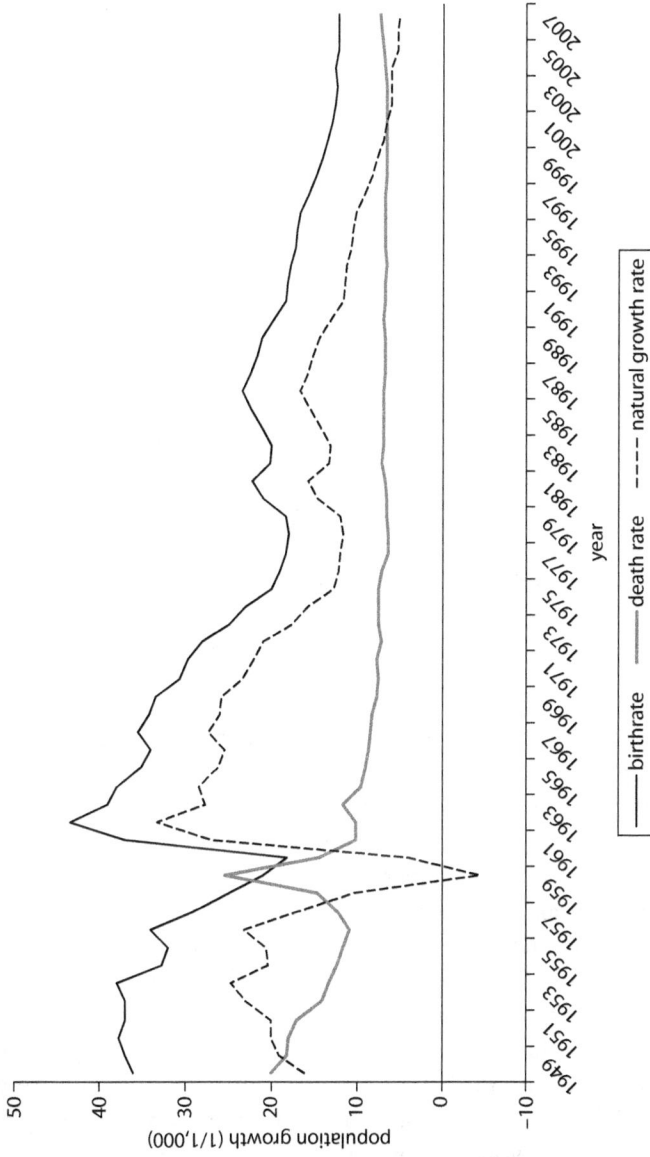

Sources: NBS 2009; Yao and Yin 1994.

Figure 1.2   International Comparison of TFRs, 1950–2010

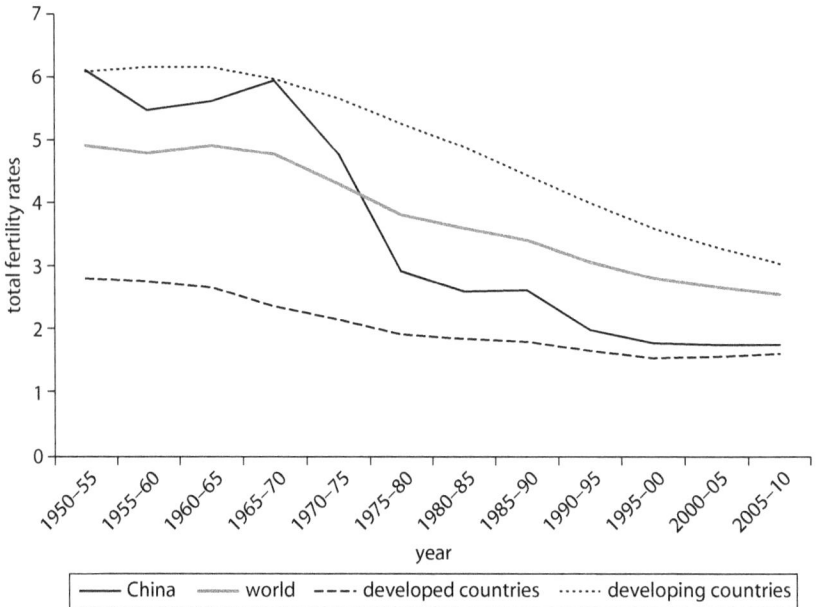

Source: UN DESA 2009; see also http://esa.un.org/unpd/wpp/index.htm.
Note: TFRs for developing countries exclude China.

been widening. In 1982, the proportion of the population 60 and older was 7.8 percent in rural and 7.1 percent in urban areas but rose to 13.7 percent and 12.1 percent, respectively, by 2005. The difference in the proportions of the population 65 and older between rural and urban areas has shown a similar trend over time.

Because rural migrants to urban areas tend to be younger than rural residents remaining behind, the increase in the elderly share of the rural population is driven by rural-to-urban migration. Latest estimates show 225.4 million rural migrants in 2008, with 62.4 percent living outside their home townships (NBS 2009), and the 2006 agricultural census found that 82.1 percent of rural migrants are younger than 40. The increase in rural-to-urban migration, especially the outflow of the rural young population, has caused acute changes in rural population pyramids in the reform era. As shown in figure 1.5, the rural population pyramid in 1982 had a larger population base, but it has narrowed significantly since then, showing a larger proportion of elderly by 2005.

Box 1.1

International Experiences on Aging and Pension Systems: How Does China Compare?

Compared with developed countries, China still has a low old-age dependency ratio, but it has risen quickly in recent years. The projected growth in the old-age dependency ratios in rural areas of China by 2030 resembles that of Japan in the past 30 years. Of the countries shown in the accompanying figure, all had comprehensive rural pension systems in place at an earlier stage of population aging than did China. In terms of social security, Denmark was the first country in the world to establish a rural pension system, in 1891. The United Kingdom started to provide pensions for rural people in 1946, and the United States in 1936. In Asia, Japan and the Republic of Korea established their rural pension systems in 1971 and 1990, respectively. The experience of developed countries suggests that preparation for aging societies includes support for the rural elderly in the process of socioeconomic transformation.

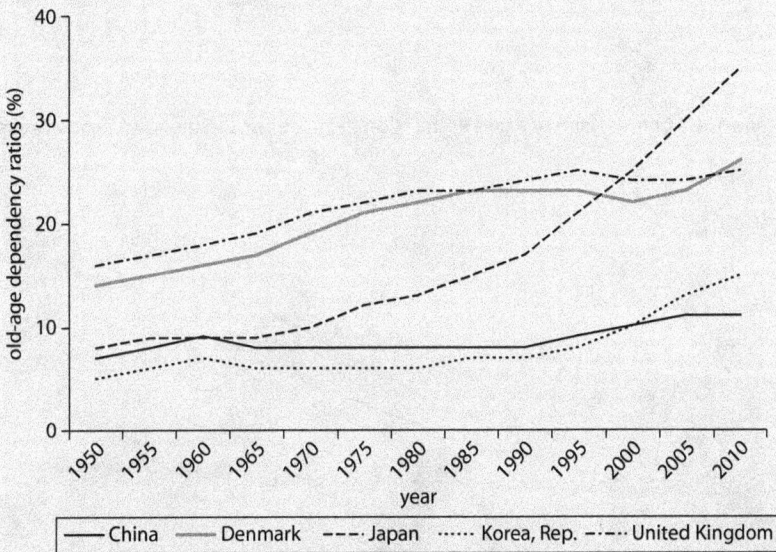

The old-age dependency ratio has also been consistently higher in rural areas because of rapid population aging. Figure 1.6 compares old-age dependency ratios in rural and urban areas. In 1982, rural and urban old-age dependency ratios were 8.4 percent and 6.6 percent, respectively. In 2005, they were 13.9 percent and 11.8 percent, respectively.

Figure 1.3   Trend of Population Aging in China, 1953–2005

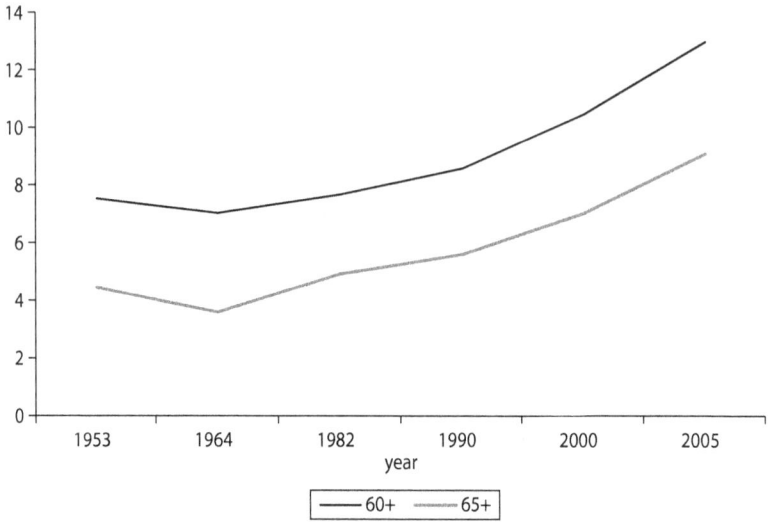

Sources: NBS 2008, 2007b, 2001; Yao and Yin 1994.

Figure 1.4   Comparison of Aged Population Proportions in Rural and Urban Areas

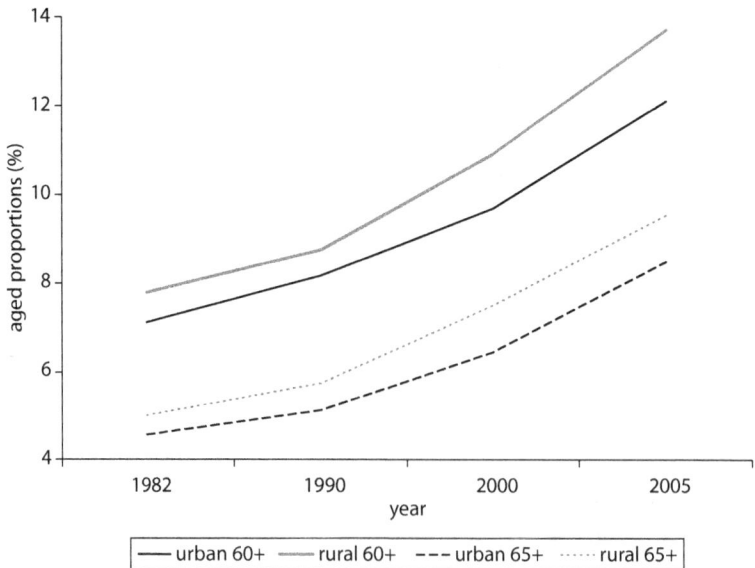

Sources: NBS 2008, 2007b, 2001; Yao and Yin 1994.

Figure 1.5   Changes in Rural Population Pyramids between 1982 and 2005

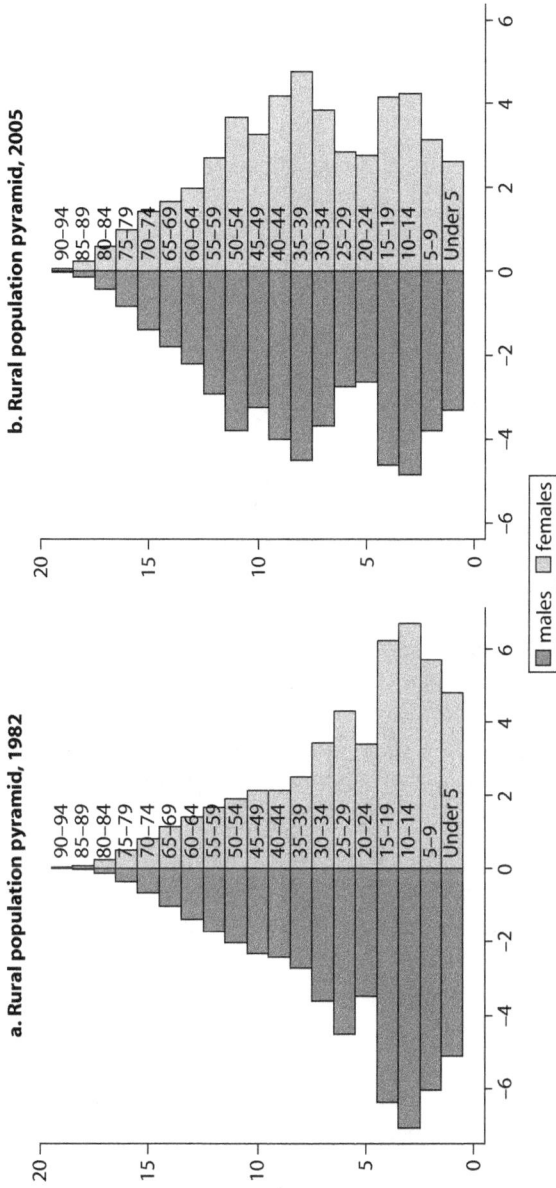

a. Rural population pyramid, 1982

b. Rural population pyramid, 2005

males   females

Source: Cai, Giles, and Wang 2009.

Figure 1.6   Comparison of Rural and Urban Old-Age Dependency Ratios

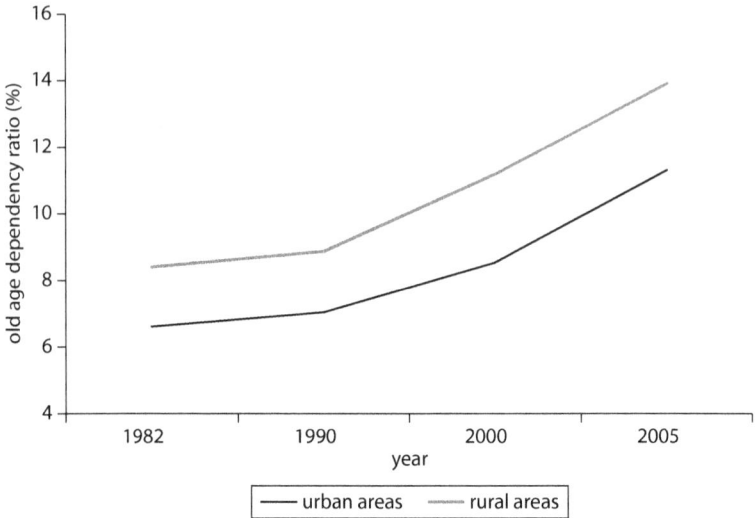

Sources: NBS 2008, 2007b, 2001; Yao and Yin 1994.

Looking Ahead—Projecting Population Trends

Although different assumptions lead to variations in the projected rate of change, China's demographic trends will continue, with an acceleration of population aging in coming years. Figure 1.5 shows the rapid historical transition in the composition of China's rural elderly population from the early 1980s to the mid-2000s. On the basis of projections completed for this report and shown in figure 1.7, this trend will continue steadily until 2030 and beyond, when the population now in their thirties and forties reaches pensionable age. The overall projected population structure is based on key variables that are discussed in the following paragraphs.

The true TFR in China has been the cause of considerable debate (Guo 2004, 2008; Retherford and others 2005). The annual population survey results show that TFRs have declined from 2.25 in 1990 to 1.45 in 2007 (figure 1.8), but these results are thought to be underestimates caused by unreported children and biased sampling. After using data from the population census and population sample to correct these estimates, the adjusted TFR is higher, at 1.57 in 2007 and close to the assumed low-fertility-rate scenario introduced below (see box 1.2 for details).

Figure 1.7 Changes in Rural Population Pyramids between 2020 and 2030

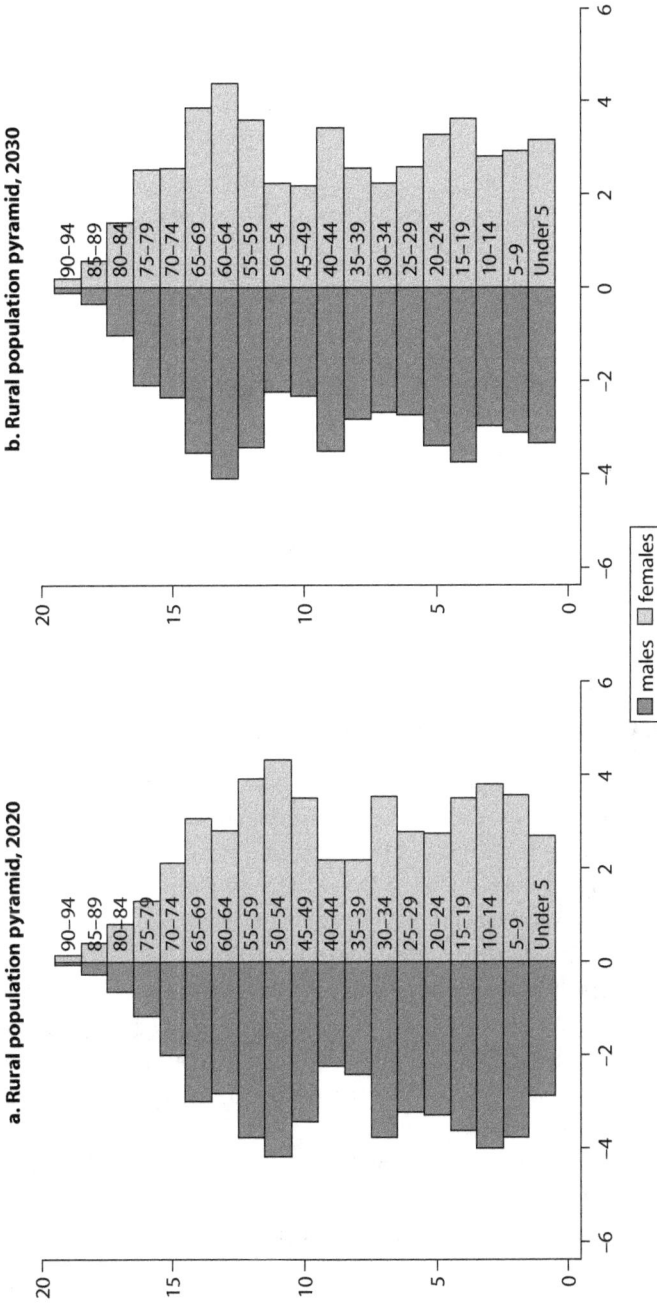

a. Rural population pyramid, 2020

b. Rural population pyramid, 2030

■ males ☐ females

Source: Cai, Giles, and Wang 2009.
Note: Fertility = 1.8 and proportion of urban population = 60 percent.

Figure 1.8   Surveyed and Adjusted TFRs in China

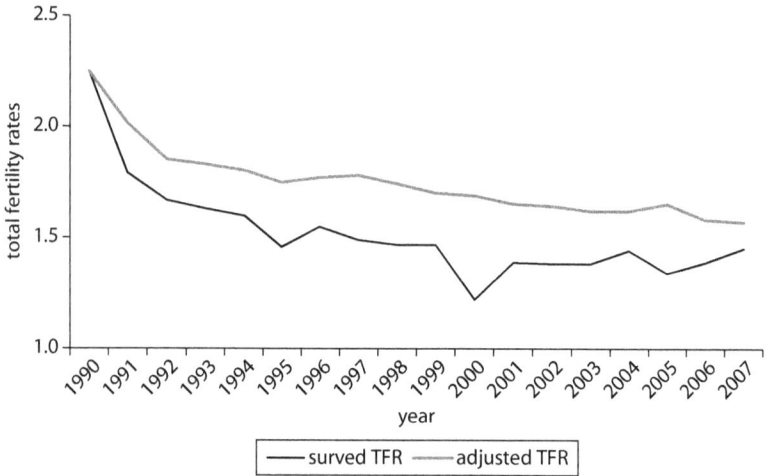

Sources: TFRs are from various surveyed data from NBS 1991–2006, 2007a, 2008; the adjusted TFRs are calculated with the supplement of census data and population sample data.

Box 1.2

Representative Population Projections in China

Several representative population projections have been developed to predict trends of China's total population. The following organizations have made different projections: the United Nations Population Division, China's Population and Family Planning Commission, Peking University, and a joint team from the Institute of Population and Labor Economics at the Chinese Academy of Social Sciences (CASS-IPLE), NBS, and the World Bank (CASS-IPLE/NBS/WB). Key parameters in population projections made by the CASS-IPLE/NBS/WB team include TFRs, life expectancy, and urbanization. Different assumptions behind these parameters produce different trends for China's total population, but these assumptions were made to serve different objectives, and the different population projections have their individual strengths and weaknesses.

The United Nations Population Division focuses on global population trends by projecting the trend of each country at the national level. It updates its population projection annually. The latest projection can be obtained from the

(continued next page)

Box 1.2 (*continued*)

2010 revision of its population database. Total fertility rates for China have four variants: 1.31 (low), 1.56 (medium), 1.81 (high), and 1.64 (constant) at the starting point. Its life expectancy assumption of 84.2 years is the same in 2100 across different scenarios. It does not assume differences in TFRs between rural and urban areas or take into account migration and urbanization.

China's Population and Family Planning Commission has made population projections similar to those of the United Nations. The projection is also based on the national level with different variants of TFRs.

The population projection of Peking University is unique. It adopts "progressive total fertility rates" instead of TFRs to make population projections. This method takes into account the differences in behavior of women who have given birth and those who have not. It also takes account of urbanization trends by using statistics on agricultural and nonagricultural population and assumes that the nonagricultural proportion of the population would be 42.9 percent in 2030 and 55.00 percent in 2050—assumptions that are obviously very low.

The joint CASS/NBS/WB population projection used in this report has the following features:

- It uses the 2000 population census and 2005 1 percent population sample to adjust TFRs in both rural and urban areas.
- It uses the classification of rural and urban areas in the 2000 population census and the 2005 population sample and makes the corresponding population projections.
- It uses two TFR scenarios: low (1.60 overall, based on 1.70 for the rural population and 1.33 for urban population) and high (1.80 overall, with rural of 2.35, urban of 1.36). For the projections presented in this chapter, the low fertility rate is used unless otherwise indicated, because it appears to be closest to what is observed from the census.
- Three levels of urbanization appear by 2030: low (55 percent), medium (60 percent), and high (65 percent). For the projections in this chapter, the medium urbanization rate is used unless otherwise indicated.
- Life expectancy is assumed to be the same as in the United Nations population projection.

Source: Cai, Giles, and Wang 2009.

If one uses the combination of low fertility rate and medium urbanization level, China's total population will continue an upward trend, but with a decreasing growth rate, peaking in 2030 at 1.41 billion. The number of working-age people will decline after 2016, earlier than the growth of total population, which will lead to a decreasing working-age to elderly support ratio. Changes in support ratios differ in rural and urban areas. The proportion of working-age people in rural areas will drop from 69.0 percent in 2008 to 63.5 percent in 2030, while the urban working-age share will decrease from 77.2 percent to 70.0 percent during the same period (figure 1.9). In the process of urbanization, migration of young people into cities will shift the distribution of the working-age population further from rural to urban areas. Among the total working-age population, rural people accounted for 51.6 percent in 2008, but that percentage will drop to 37.7 percent in 2030 under reasonable rural-to-urban migration assumptions.

Even with higher TFRs in rural areas, migration implies that population aging will occur more rapidly in rural areas. In 2008, 9.35 percent of the population was 65 years of age and older in rural areas and 6.94 percent in urban areas, a gap of 2.41 percentage points. By 2030, the aged proportions in rural and urban areas will be 21.84 percent and 14.75 percent, respectively, increasing the gap to 7.09 percentage points (figure 1.10). As more young people move to and choose to stay in

Figure 1.9   Trends of Working-Age Population in China, 2008–30

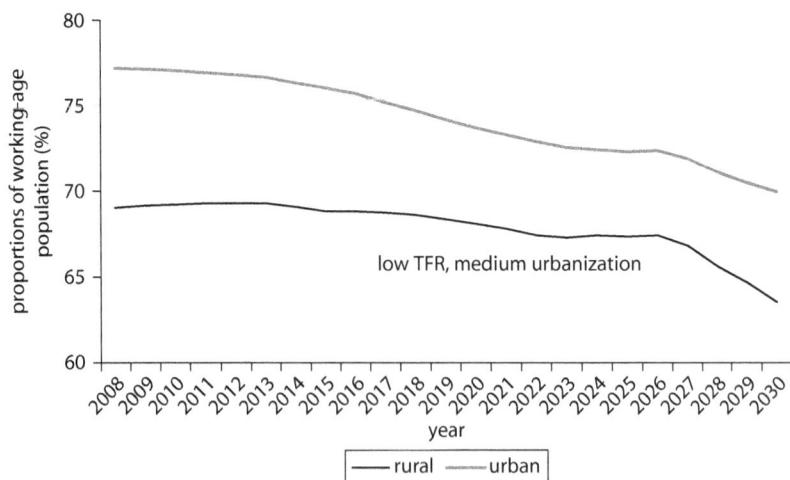

Source: Cai, Giles, and Wang 2009.

Figure 1.10   Trends of Population Aging in Rural and Urban China, 2008–30

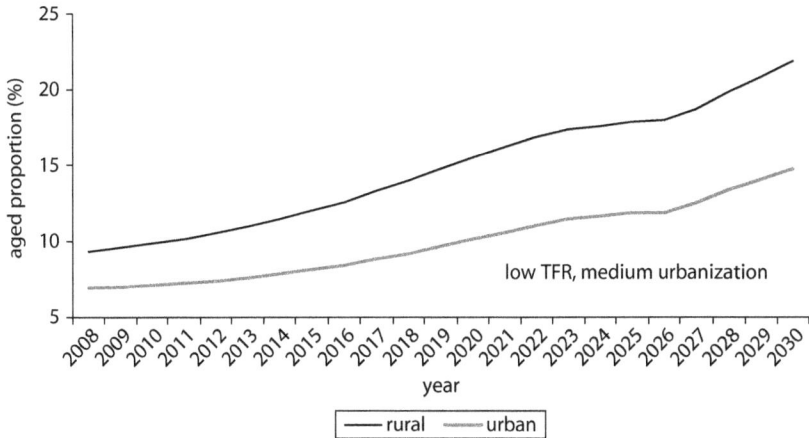

Source: Cai, Giles, and Wang 2009.

cities, finding favorable conditions in rural areas to support the rural elderly poses a major challenge to China's rural and socioeconomic transformation.

The acceleration of population aging will raise the support burden of the working-age population, though this effect will be masked somewhat in the medium term by a decline in the child dependency ratio in rural areas. The total dependency ratios in rural areas appear stable between 2008 and 2025 (figure 1.11) because the rural child dependency ratio will fall significantly while the pace of population aging increases. The child dependency ratios will converge between rural and urban areas in 2025 and then remain stable. The child dependency ratio in urban areas will keep increasing, but at a slower pace.

Old-age dependency ratios will diverge between rural and urban areas (figure 1.12). In 2008, rural and urban ratios were 13.5 percent and 9.0 percent, respectively, and the gap was 4.5 percentage points. The gap in old-age dependency ratios will widen to 13.3 percentage points by 2030, when the old-age dependency ratio will reach 34.4 percent in rural areas and 21.1 percent in urban areas.

Although different assumed scenarios for urbanization and fertility yield somewhat differing results, the fundamental demographic trends remain similar. Figure 1.13 reports the elderly shares of the rural population under four combinations of TFRs and 2030 urbanization levels to test the robustness of the conclusions under the "base case" scenario used

Figure 1.11   Trends of Total Dependency Ratios in Rural and Urban China, 2008–30

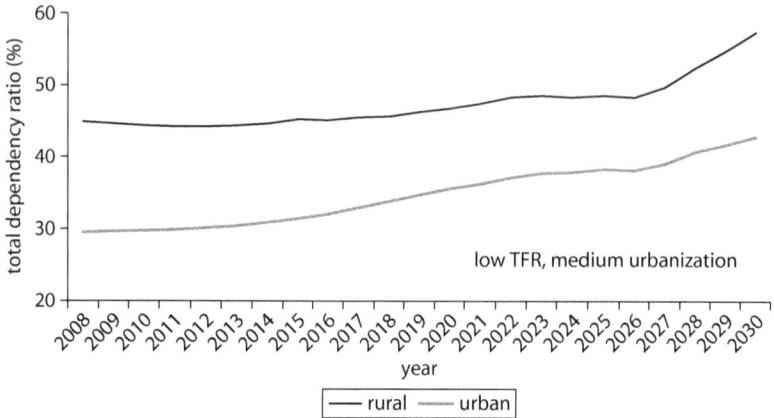

low TFR, medium urbanization

Source: Cai, Giles, and Wang 2009.

Figure 1.12   Old-Age Dependency Ratios in Rural and Urban China, 2008–30

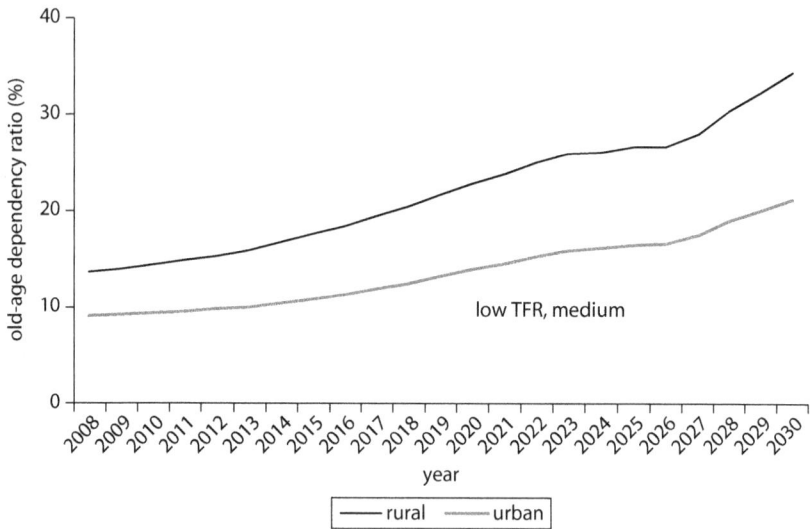

low TFR, medium

Source: Cai, Giles, and Wang 2009.

in this report of low TFR and medium urbanization. The four combinations are as follows:

• High TFR and high urbanization level
• High TFR and low urbanization level

Figure 1.13   Scenarios of Aged Proportions in Rural China, 2008–30

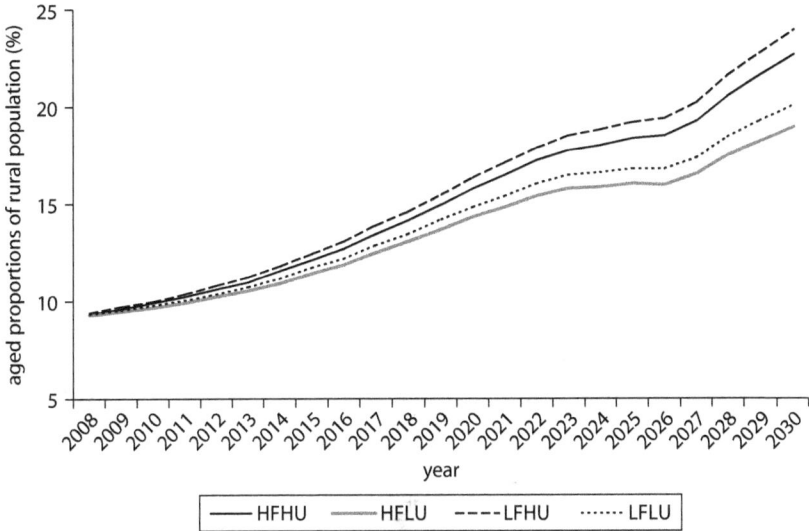

Source: Cai, Giles, and Wang 2009.
Note: HFHU = high TFR, high urbanization level; HFLU = high TFR, low urbanization level; LFHU = low TFR, high urbanization level; LFLU = low TFR, low urbanization level.

- Low TFR and high urbanization level
- Low TFR and low urbanization level

The trends from the preceding four combinations are similar, but the elderly proportions of rural population differ significantly under each scenario by 2030.

As shown in figure 1.13, the largest aged proportion occurs under a scenario of low TFR and high urbanization level by 2030. As discussed before, migration will attract more young people into cities. In the meantime, the low TFR will accelerate the speed of population aging. Therefore, these two forces will influence population aging in rural areas. In contrast, the smallest aged proportion would occur in the scenario with high TFR and low urbanization. With more young people staying in rural areas, the aged proportion would be lower. In 2030, the difference in the aged proportion between these two scenarios is 3.9 percentage points. Urbanization will likely accelerate in the coming years. The scenario of low TFR and high urbanization is therefore perfectly possible and would result in the most acute dependency ratio in rural areas (figure 1.14).

Figure 1.14   Scenarios of Old-Age Dependency Ratios in Rural China, 2008–30

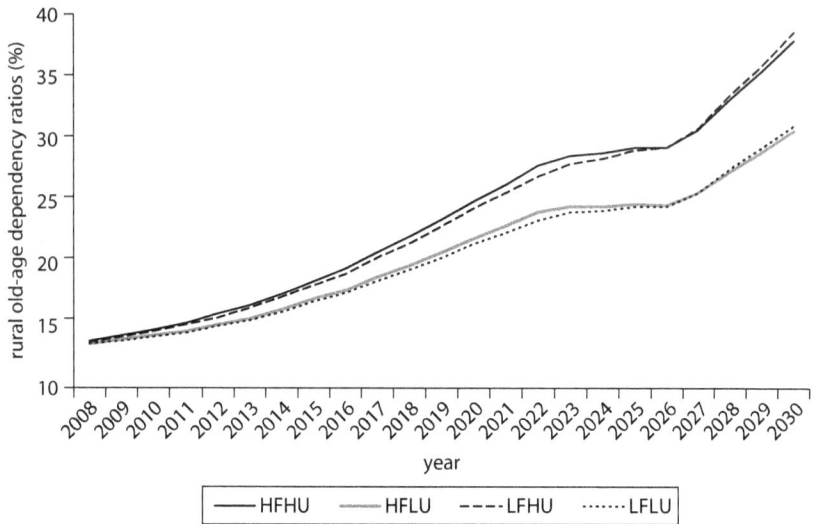

Source: Cai, Giles, and Wang 2009.
Note: HFHU = high TFR, high urbanization level; HFLU = high TFR, low urbanization level; LFHU = low TFR, high urbanization level; LFLU = low TFR, low urbanization level.

Conclusion

As the demographic transition outlined in this chapter takes place, families will suffer further strain to support future generations of the rural elderly when young adults move into cities and family size becomes smaller, with fewer potential care providers. The population projections in this chapter use different fertility and migration scenarios to illustrate the acceleration of the demographic transition; they show that aging will remain far more pronounced in rural than urban areas. Although fertility is higher in rural areas than in urban areas, the large-scale migration of the young population will hollow out villages and leave behind older people, women, and children. At the national level, the old-age dependency ratio will pass 20 percent and continue to rise even faster to 30 percent around 2028. The levels of old-age dependency will be significantly higher in rural areas, and the gap in dependency rates between rural and urban areas will widen.

The trends of population aging in rural areas raise many questions about the potential for future elderly to support themselves and the possibility that they may fall into poverty. To address these questions, the current determinants of poverty and sources of formal and informal support among the elderly are examined, including the following: How much poverty and vulnerability are observed presently among the rural elderly, and is this situation changing over time? What kinds of formal and informal social protection methods are available for rural households to cope with (and forestall) poverty among the rural elderly? What effects has the mass migration of recent years had on the efficacy of informal social protection mechanisms? In light of the evidence, does public policy have a role to support the rural aged population? The following chapters address these questions.

Note

1. See World Bank (forthcoming) for discussion of other strains on traditional support networks and chapters 3 and 4 of this report for sources of support and savings for the rural elderly.

References

Cai, Fang, John Giles, and Dewen Wang. 2009. "The Well-Being of China's Rural Elderly." Background Paper for East Asia Social Protection Team, World Bank, Washington, DC.

Gu, Baochang, Wang Feng, Guo Zhigang, and Zhang Erli. 2007. "China's Local and National Fertility Policies at the End of the Twentieth Century." *Population and Development Review* 33 (1): 129–47.

Guo, Zhigang. 2004. "A Study and Discussion on China's Fertility in the 1990s." [In Chinese.] *Population Research* 28 (2): 10–19.

———. 2008. "China's Low Fertility and Its Determinants," *Population Research* 32 (4): 1–12.

Johnson, D. Gale. 1994. "Effects of Institutions and Policies on Rural Population Growth with Application to China." *Population and Development Review* 20 (3): 503–31.

NBS (National Bureau of Statistics). 1991–2006. *China Population Statistics Yearbook*. Beijing: China Statistics Press.

———. 2001. *2000 Fifth Population Census Data*. Beijing: China Statistics Press.

———. 2007a. *China Population and Employment Statistics Yearbook*. Beijing: China Statistics Press.

———. 2007b. "2005 One Percent Population Sample Dataset" (unpublished).

———. 2008. *China Population and Employment Statistics Yearbook*. Beijing: China Statistics Press.

———. 2009. *China Population and Employment Statistics Yearbook*. Beijing: China Statistics Press.

Retherford, D. Robert, Minja Kim Choe, Jiajian Chen, Xiru Li, and Hongyan Cui, 2005. "How Far Has Fertility in China Really Declined?" *Population and Development Review* 31 (1): 57–84.

Schultz, T. Paul, and Zeng Yi. 1999. "The Impact of Institutional Reform from 1979 through 1987 on Fertility in Rural China." *China Economic Review* 10: 141–60.

Uhlenberg, Peter. 2009. *International Handbook of Population Aging*. New York: Springer.

UN DESA (United Nations, Department of Economic and Social Affairs, Population Division). 2009. "World Population Prospects: The 2008 Revision, Highlights." ESA/P/WP.210. New York: United Nations. http://www.un.org/esa/population/publications/wpp2008/wpp2008_text_tables.pdf.

Vermeer, Eduard B. 2006. "Demographic Dimensions of China's Development." *Population and Development Review* 32: 115–44.

World Bank. Forthcoming. *Social Assistance in Rural China: Tackling Poverty through Rural Dibao*. Washington, DC: World Bank.

Yao, Xinwu, and Hua Yin. 1994. *China Normally Used Population Dataset*. Beijing: China Population Press.

CHAPTER 2

Poverty and Vulnerability among China's Rural Elderly

This chapter looks at poverty and vulnerability among the rural elderly in China during the past decade. Key findings include the following:

- The rural elderly are on average poorer than the general population and substantially poorer than the urban elderly.
- They are also more likely to remain poor and are more vulnerable than the younger population.
- Location matters more as a determinant of poverty for the rural elderly than for working-age adults, though its importance has declined over time.
- In terms of factors that affect incomes of the rural elderly, those who have more education or a pension are likely to have higher incomes. The effect of having a migrant child is, however, more complex. Although having a migrant child has an inconclusive effect on the income of elderly rural households, having migrant children has a clearer and positive effect in terms of ability to cope with shocks to household income, whether communitywide or household specific.

Poverty among the Rural Elderly

As a group, the rural elderly remain notably poorer than younger rural households, even though their poverty rates have fallen over recent decades. Figure 2.1 highlights this situation by showing the evolution of the rural poverty head-count ratio by age of household head from 1991 to 2004.[1] Income poverty has fallen for all age groups in rural China, but notably, households headed by older individuals have a higher incidence of poverty than households with working-age heads for each year. By 2004, the income poverty rate for rural households with working-age heads was only 8.5 percent, whereas it was 15.0 percent for households with a head age 71 to 80 years and 17.0 percent for households with a head over 80 years of age. This pattern occurs because younger working-age adults with higher education are more likely to take advantage of opportunities from economic growth.

The rural elderly have also remained consistently poorer than the urban elderly over time. Using the China Urban and Rural Elderly Survey (CURES) conducted in 2006, table 2.1 provides a comparison of poverty among the elderly in urban and rural areas. Poverty among the elderly is a much greater problem in rural than in urban areas. The CURES (2006),[2] which is a nationally representative sample, suggests that 19 percent of rural elderly have consumption levels below the official poverty line, whereas only 6 percent of the urban elderly are below the higher "basic needs line." The comparable share of elderly with consumption below the basic needs line in rural areas is 29 percent. The poverty gap measure, which measures the depth of households below the poverty line, also suggests a more severe problem in rural areas than in urban areas. Finally, the poverty severity measure picks up the effects of inequality among the poor and suggests that severe poverty is also a more serious problem in rural than urban areas.[3] Given the access of the urban elderly to pension income as well as family support, it is not surprising that poverty is much higher among the rural elderly.

Chronic Poverty among the Rural Elderly

Chronic, or persistent, poverty is also a problem faced more by older rural households. The *chronically poor* can be defined as those households that are poor on three successive survey rounds. Households headed by elderly individuals in their seventies remain the most exposed to chronic poverty. Although incidence of chronic income poverty fell in the China Health

Figure 2.1 Percentage of Poor Rural Households, by Age of Household Head

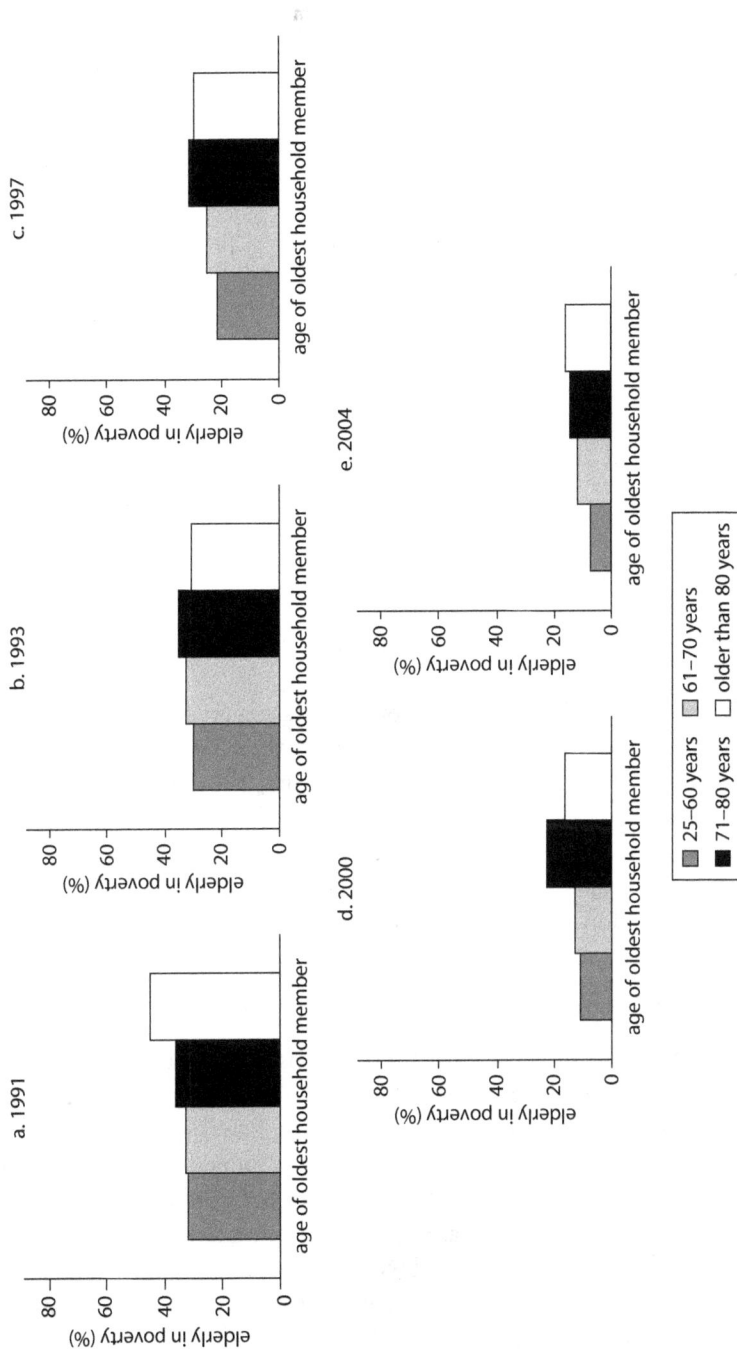

a. 1991

elderly in poverty (%)

age of oldest household member

b. 1993

elderly in poverty (%)

age of oldest household member

c. 1997

elderly in poverty (%)

age of oldest household member

d. 2000

elderly in poverty (%)

age of oldest household member

e. 2004

elderly in poverty (%)

age of oldest household member

- 25–60 years
- 71–80 years
- 61–70 years
- older than 80 years

Sources: CHNS 1991, 1993, 1997, 2000, 2004.

Table 2.1   Measuring the Poverty of the Rural and Urban Elderly
share of population under line

	Income poverty			Consumption poverty		
	Head-count index	Poverty gap	Poverty severity	Head-count index	Poverty gap	Poverty severity
Rural elderly						
Official poverty line	0.196	0.083	0.044	0.192	0.075	0.040
Basic needs line	0.287	0.127	0.073	0.287	0.118	0.067
One-dollar-a-day line	0.303	0.131	0.076	0.292	0.123	0.070
Urban elderly						
Basic needs line	0.054	0.020	0.013	0.058	0.027	0.018
One-dollar-a-day line	0.034	0.017	0.012	0.055	0.025	0.016

Source: Cai, Giles, and Park 2009, estimated using data from CURES 2006.

and Nutrition Survey (CHNS) to nearly zero for cohorts under 70 years of age, nearly 22 percent of elderly in their seventies as of 2000 experienced persistent poverty over three survey rounds spanning a seven-year period (figure 2.2).

Why do rural elderly in their seventies face a greater incidence of persistent income poverty? Younger elderly in their sixties continue to earn considerable income from work in agriculture, but the ability to continue agricultural work degrades with age, and the elderly lack significant sources of income other than support from adult children. Those elderly surviving into their eighties are a select group. In rural areas, they typically reside with adult children, who have higher incomes.

Vulnerability to Poverty

Vulnerability to poverty over time is considerably higher than actual poverty at any one point in time. Following an approach used in the World Bank's China poverty assessment (Chaudhuri and Datt 2009), this book determines a household to be vulnerable to poverty if it is poor in one of three survey years over a six-year period. Figure 2.3 shows the share of the rural population vulnerable to poverty during early and late periods of the CHNS panel (1991 to 1997, and 1997 to 2004).[4] Because rural incomes are quite variable, the probability that a household experiences negative shocks and incomes below the poverty

Figure 2.2   Share of Rural Elderly Households Experiencing Chronic Poverty

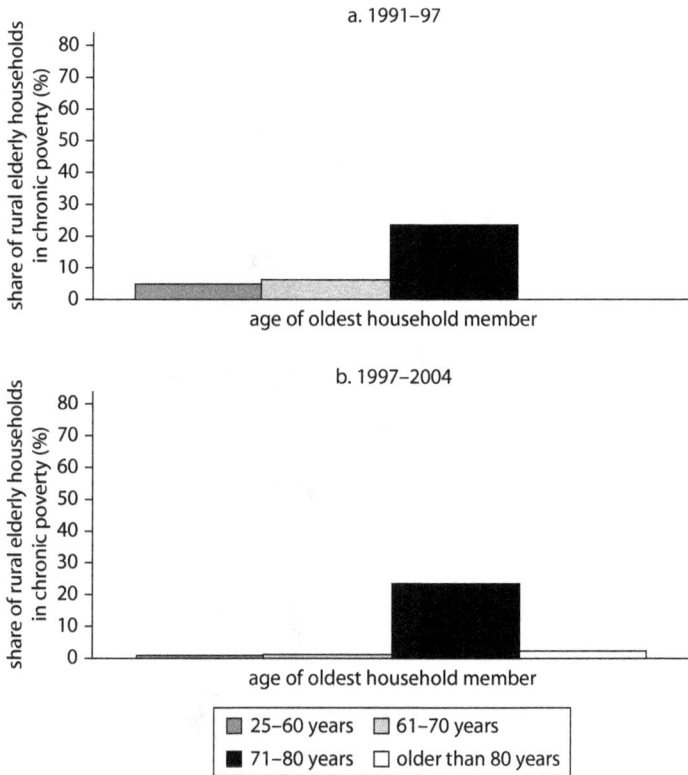

a. 1991–97

b. 1997–2004

25–60 years   61–70 years
71–80 years   older than 80 years

Sources: CHNS 1991, 1993, 1997, 2000, 2004.
Note: A household is determined to be chronically poor if it has income below the poverty level in each of three survey rounds of the designated period. The incidence of vulnerability is calculated by the age of the oldest household member in 1993 for the 1991–97 period and in 2000 for the 1997–2004 period.

line in one year of a six-year period will be higher than annual income poverty rates.[5]

Rural households with older heads are more vulnerable to poverty, and declines in vulnerability between 1991 and 2004 have been more pronounced for households headed by working-age individuals and least pronounced for households headed by individuals in their seventies. Nearly 63 percent of households headed by an individual in his or her seventies in 2000 experienced income below the basic needs line in 1997, 2000, or 2004. This occurred for fewer than 40 percent of working-age adults and only 45 percent of households headed by

Figure 2.3   Share of Rural Elderly Households Vulnerable to Poverty

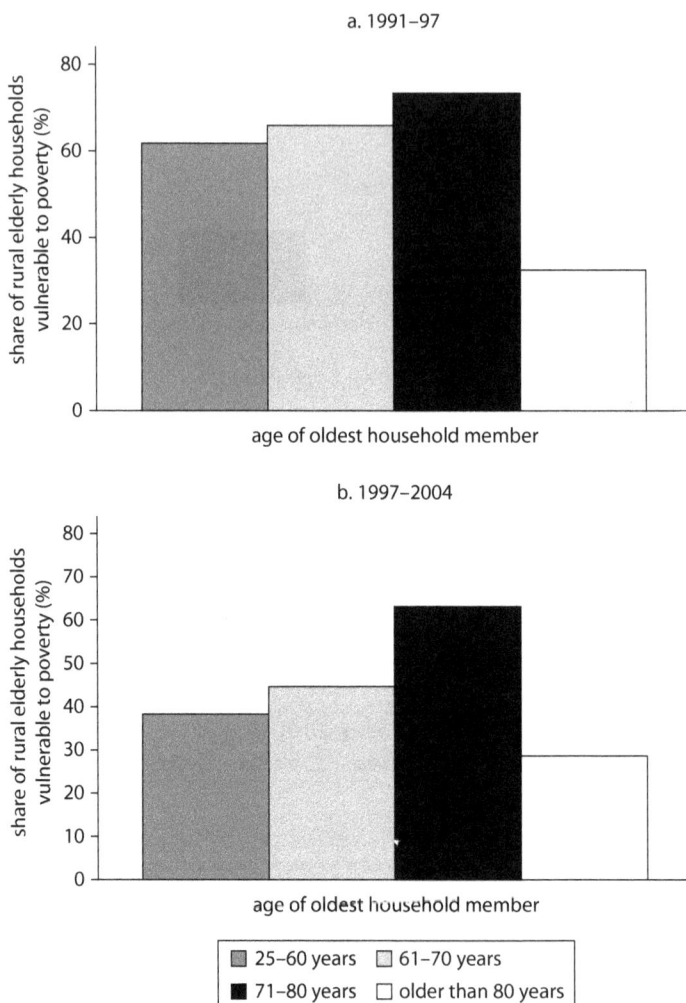

a. 1991–97

b. 1997–2004

| ▨ 25–60 years | ☐ 61–70 years |
| ■ 71–80 years | ☐ older than 80 years |

Source: CHNS 1991, 1993, 1997, 2000, 2004.
Note: Vulnerability occurs if a household's income falls below the poverty level in at least one of three years. The incidence of vulnerability is calculated by the age of the oldest household member in 1993 for the 1991–97 period and in 2000 for the 1997–2004 period.

someone in their sixties. Vulnerability was also fairly low among households with heads in their eighties, probably because rural residents in their eighties nearly always coreside with younger family members. "Head of household" in these cases more likely reflects ownership of the dwelling and not primary income earner status in the household.

The Geographic Dimension of Poverty

The importance of location as a determinant of poverty has declined for all households since the 1990s, but the decline is higher in absolute terms for households headed by elderly people. Early in the reform era, spatial differences in incomes and poverty incidence were largely driven by restrictions on migration reinforced by differences in per capita land endowments, access to urban markets, and level of local development. With China's economic reform, the importance of geography has declined in explaining poverty and inequality (Benjamin, Brandt, and Giles 2005), while inequality within communities was increasing at an even faster rate as individuals differed in their ability to take advantage of wider off-farm labor markets with migration. Young adult migrants may provide support to elderly parents through remittances, so one might observe that geography becomes less important for explaining inequality and poverty among the elderly. In table 2.2, results show a decline in the share of variance in income that can be explained by village location from 1993 to 2000, with a slight increase after 2004 for all households and for households with elderly, respectively.[6] The degree to which location explains variation in poverty status declined from 26 percent in 1991 to 12 percent in 2004. The decline in importance of location in explaining poverty reflects the importance of increasing market integration as a means of raising incomes for households in villages that were previously isolated.

When one looks at households with elderly residents, location obviously was more important in earlier years for explaining both volatility of income and poverty status. Also, the importance of location in determining poverty status among the elderly declined even more sharply, from 40 percent to 20 percent, between 1993 and 2004. This finding suggests that even if the rural elderly are unable to directly benefit from

Table 2.2   Role of Village Location in Determining Poverty of China's Rural Elderly
share of variance explained by village location

Dependent variable to decompose	1991	1993	1997	2000	2004
All households					
ln(income per capita)	0.279	0.301	0.264	0.258	0.262
Poverty	0.256	0.263	0.213	0.147	0.124
Households with elderly					
ln(income per capita)	0.381	0.421	0.381	0.355	0.301
Poverty	0.358	0.400	0.301	0.242	0.200

Source: Cai, Giles, and Wang 2009, estimated using CHNS 1991, 1993, 1997, 2000, and 2004.

employment in distant markets, they enjoy some spillover benefits as family members remit incomes earned as migrant workers.

Nonetheless, location remains a stronger determinant of welfare among the rural elderly than among all rural households. The fact that 20 percent of the variation in elderly poverty status can be explained by village location as late as 2004 suggests that, relative to working-age adults, elderly persons remaining in home villages are less likely to have benefited from the increase in opportunities resulting from China's economic reforms.[7]

Income Determinants of the Elderly

Apart from geography, the incomes of the elderly may vary with common shocks experienced by the community, with their own health status or the health status of other household residents, and with the migration status of adult children. Indeed, a growing literature on migration in China shows how migration has contributed to raising the incomes of rural households and facilitated smoothing the effects of shocks to income.[8] The rural elderly may not benefit from increases in rural-to-urban migration if the elderly are members of poorer households that are less involved in migrant employment or if migrant children are not remitting a share of their income.

The results in table 2.3 highlight the effects of three policy variables on household income per capita: human capital (the average education of adult household members), formal social support (whether a family member receives a pension), and migration (whether the adult child of the household from a previous round is now working elsewhere as a migrant). The main findings in this regard follow.

- *Increasing the average education of adult members of elderly households by one year is associated with a 7.6 percent increase in income per capita.* Thus, higher human capital among adults in a household may improve not only the well-being of working-age adults but also the well-being of their elderly parents.
- *Receipt of a pension is associated with 67 percent higher household income per capita.* In observing the correlation between pension receipt and household income, however, one must remember that few households in rural areas received pensions at the time of the surveys and that receipt of a pension was likely to be correlated with other household characteristics that lead to higher incomes (for example, high human capital, prior military service, or experience as a village cadre).

Table 2.3   Factors Affecting Income per Capita of Households with Elderly
dependent variable: ln(hh income per capita)

Model	1	2
Average years of education of adult household members	0.076*** (0.007)	0.076*** (0.009)
Has family members with pension income	0.692*** (0.037)	0.671*** (0.043)
Has migrant family members	0.057 (0.060)	0.061 (0.073)
Community income shock		0.156*** (0.028)
(Community income shock)* (Migrant family members)		−0.126** (0.064)
Elder died in the following year		−0.374*** (0.094)
(Elder died following year)* (Migrant family members)		1.008*** (0.376)
R-squared	0.203	0.190
Number of observations	5,060	3,708

Source: Cai, Giles, and Wang 2009, estimated using CHNS 1991, 1993, 1997, 2000, 2004, and 2006.
Note: Migrant family member = a member of the household from a previous round is no longer a household member and is currently working as a migrant.
Community income shock = change in log income per capita for all other households in the enumeration area.
All models also include years of education, age, age-squared, lives with spouse, lives with adult children, number of adult household members, year dummy variables, and enumeration area dummy variables. The model number shown above corresponds to the model number in the expanded set of results.
Standard errors of model coefficients are shown in parentheses.
*, **, and *** indicate significance of 10, 5, and 1 percent, respectively.

- *The effect of having a migrant family member suggests a 5.7 percent increase in income, but this effect is statistically insignificant.* This result is somewhat surprising, so one must examine further whether having a migrant family member is significant at times of communitywide shocks.

Although the effect of having a migrant household member on household income is inconclusive, a migrant child provides insurance against loss of income stemming from shocks to the local economy. As shown in table 2.3, the coefficient for the interaction between the occurrence of a community income shock and having a migrant adult child in the household is significantly negative, indicating that having a migrant child can mitigate the effects of a communitywide shock.

Another major source of shock to incomes comes from illness, either to oneself or to another elderly member of the household. Health status can be captured using objective measures, such as activities of daily living or body mass index, but a stronger indication of the likelihood that a household member has been incapacitated is subsequent mortality. Typically, individuals who die experience periods of incapacitation a year or two before passing away. This analysis therefore uses death of a household member one year following a survey round as a proxy for the presence of a family member who is too ill to work and examines the impact on household income.[9]

The effects of ill health of the elderly on household income are substantial but are more than compensated for where households have absent migrant members, because of transfers from these migrant household members. Households experience a 37 percent drop in income per capita in the year before the death of an elderly resident. This drop is likely driven by the lost earnings of the incapacitated family member and other family members who provide care to that person. For households with a migrant family member, however, an *increase* in income of 65 percent occurs in such circumstances. When households have a migrant family member and a resident suffers from a serious illness, migrant children contribute sufficient funds to reduce lost earned income of the household and to support additional expenditures related to health care.

Although migrant children help smooth the effects of shocks to income and health, these effects might be predominantly experienced by households either below or above the poverty line. To examine whether insurance against shocks affects transitions into poverty, the analysis examined how shocks and migration status affect the probability that a household falls below the poverty line (table 2.4).[10] The findings are as follows:

- *Raising the average education of adult members of the household by one year leads to a 6 percent decline in the probability that a household is in poverty.*
- *Those households in which a family member has pension income are 58 percent less likely to be in poverty.*
- *Elderly households with migrant family members are 26 percent less likely to have incomes below the poverty line.* When this result is contrasted with the negligible effect of migrant family members on income levels shown in table 2.3, it suggests that migrant family members may play an important role in keeping households out of poverty even if they do not raise incomes much above this threshold. Although they may not boost income for the average household, they may play an important role in raising incomes of households that would otherwise fall below the poverty line.

Table 2.4   Factors Affecting Likelihood of Household Poverty of the Elderly, Marginal Effects from Probit Model

dependent variable: household below poverty = 1

Model	1	2
Average years of education of adult household members	−0.059*** (0.012)	−0.056*** (0.014)
Has family members with pension income	−0.577*** (0.066)	−0.671*** (0.082)
Has migrant family members	−0.260*** (0.084)	−0.275*** (0.106)
Community income shock		−0.140*** (0.039)
(Community income shock)* (Migrant family members)		0.048 (0.099)
Elder died in the following year		0.248** (0.124)
Number of observations	5,182	3,558

Source: Cai, Giles, and Wang 2009.
Note: Migrant family member = a member of the household from a previous round is no longer a household member and is currently working as a migrant.
Community income shock = change in log income per capita for all other households in the enumeration area.
All models also include years of education, age, age-squared, lives with spouse, lives with adult children, number of adult household members, year dummy variables, and enumeration area dummy variables. The model number shown above corresponds to the model number in the expanded set of results.
Standard errors of model coefficients are shown in parentheses.
*, **, and *** indicate significance of 10, 5, and 1 percent, respectively.

- *Migrant children may help insure against poverty generally but not provide additional insurance against poverty that is caused by communitywide shocks.* Negative shocks to the local economy raise the likelihood that a household with elderly residents will fall into poverty. This finding is evident from the results for model 2 in table 2.4, where adding a communitywide income shock suggests that a 1 percent negative income shock experienced by the community will raise the probability that a household with elderly residents will fall into poverty by 0.14 percent. In contrast to results in table 2.3, one does not observe that migrant family members yield significant insurance against the effects of communitywide shocks. This result is reflected in the low and insignificant coefficient on the community shock–migrant family member interaction term in model 2, indicating that existence of migrant family members does not appear to insure against the possibility that communitywide shocks drive households with elderly into poverty.
- *Elderly households with a resident who is seriously ill are 25 percent more likely to have incomes below the poverty line, but having migrant*

children removes this effect.[11] This finding is evident from the coefficient on the variable "elder died in the following year" in model 2 of table 2.4.

- *These estimates also suggest that migrant children eliminate the effect of serious illness on the probability of falling into poverty.* Migrant family members either return to care for elderly parents who are infirm (Giles and Mu 2007), or a migrant child is able to provide transfers sufficient to keep the family income stable when an elderly resident becomes seriously ill.

On balance, the evidence raises concerns that shocks to the local economy and serious health shocks experienced by household members affect incomes of the elderly. Given the rural pension pilot, one potential value of this formal social insurance would be to provide a base level of support that would keep China's rural elderly from falling into poverty. In principle, the rural *dibao* already plays this role, but coverage is limited and the manner in which it is targeted and implemented may further limit its effectiveness. Local village leaders responsible for targeting households to receive *dibao* support may have less skill at identifying households that suffer from transient poverty rather than chronic poverty. For older workers, transient poverty caused by a shock may quickly develop into chronic poverty because aging workers are less able to find new income-earning opportunities after falling into poverty.

Conclusion

The evidence in this chapter indicates that the rural elderly are on average poorer, more likely to remain poor, and more vulnerable than the younger population, as well as substantially poorer than the urban elderly. Location also matters more for elderly than younger adults as a determinant of poverty. In terms of the factors that affect the incomes of the rural elderly, those who have more education or a pension are likely to have higher incomes. The effect of having a migrant child is, however, more complex. Although having a migrant child has an inconclusive impact on the income of elderly rural households, having migrant children has a clearer and positive effect in terms of ability to cope with shocks to household income, whether communitywide or household specific.

Given this situation, exploring the sources of support for the rural elderly and the extent to which they can be expected to improve their lot over time—or, at a minimum, not contribute to its deterioration—is important. The following chapter looks in detail at sources of support among the rural elderly, both support from their own earnings and formal and informal sources of support other than their own work.

Notes

1. The estimates are based on the China Health and Nutrition Survey (CHNS), which is a panel data set containing the same households and individuals from 1991 through 2006. Because it does not have a good measure of total consumption, income was used to measure the poverty head count, and a household is considered to be poor if it earns less than the basic needs line (875 renminbi [RMB] in 2000 yuan). Because incomes in rural China are quite volatile, poverty rates calculated using income overstate the share of households below the poverty line; 2006 is not included because pension income was not enumerated that year, and one cannot calculate a consistent measure of income.

2. The CURES is a national representative survey that collects information on the living status and well-being of urban and rural elderly in 20 provinces.

3. The poverty severity index is Foster, Greer, and Thorbecke (1984), using a sensitivity parameter of 2.

4. For the early period, the households are grouped by age of the household head in 1993, and for the later period, by age of the head in 2000.

5. Research on consumption smoothing in China has found that households that are reasonably well-off are also capable of smoothing the effects of income shocks on consumption, whereas poorer households do less well. See Jalan and Ravallion (1999) and Giles (2006).

6. The analysis decomposes the variances of log income and poverty status to show how much of the variance is explained by village location. See Cai, Giles, and Wang (2009) for details of the calculation used in this book.

7. Although location actually explains less variation in income and poverty in 2004 than in 1993, in a fully integrated economy the contribution of location to variation in income is typically considerably lower. Benjamin and others (2008) note that within-province income inequality explains 98.5 percent of income inequality in Canada, and thus the contribution of geography to income inequality (or poverty) remains much greater in China. In other developing countries, such as India, which lack nationally integrated labor markets, one might expect that geography contributes substantially more to the probability of falling into poverty.

8. For evidence on the relationship between migration and incomes, see Du, Park, and Wang (2005) and de Brauw and Giles (2008). For a discussion of migration and risk coping, see Giles (2006) and Giles and Yoo (2007).

9. Subsequent mortality was viewed as a more reliable proxy for health status than self-reported health in early research on retirement decisions in the United States. See, for example, Anderson and Burkhauser (1985), Hurd and Boskin (1984), and Parsons (1980). Giles and Mu (2007) make use of subsequent mortality as a measure of health status in a paper examining whether parent illness affects the migration decision of adult children.

10. To do this, binary response models were estimated in which the outcome is equal to one if household income per capita falls below a basic needs poverty line (875 RMB per capita in year 2000 RMB yuan).

11. Technical difficulties complicate identifying this effect using a probit model, but the interaction term has been examined in a linear probability model.

References

Anderson, Kathryn H., and Richard V. Burkhauser. 1985. "The Retirement-Health Nexus: A New Measure of an Old Puzzle." *Journal of Human Resources* 20 (3): 315–30.

Benjamin, Dwayne, Loren Brandt, and John Giles. 2005. "The Evolution of Income Inequality in Rural China." *Economic Development and Cultural Change* 53 (4): 769–824.

Benjamin, Dwayne, Loren Brandt, John Giles, and Sangui Wang. 2008. "Income Inequality during China's Economic Transition." In *China's Great Economic Transformation*, ed. Loren Brandt and Thomas Rawski, 729–75. Cambridge: Cambridge University Press.

Cai, Fang, John Giles, and Dewen Wang. 2009. "The Well-Being of China's Rural Elderly." Background Paper for East Asia Social Protection Team, World Bank, Washington, DC.

Chaudhuri, Shubham, and Gaurav Datt. 2009. *From Poor Areas to Poor People: China's Evolving Poverty Agenda, an Assessment of Poverty and Inequality in China*, Washington, DC: World Bank.

CHNS (China Health and Nutrition Survey). Various years. China Center for Disease Control and Prevention and the Carolina Population Center, University of North Carolina at Chapel Hill. http://www.cpc.unc.edu/projects/china.

CURES (China Urban and Rural Elderly Survey). "China Urban and Rural Elderly Survey Micro-Data, 2006" (unpublished). China Research Center on Aging, Beijing.

de Brauw, Alan, and John Giles. 2008. "Migrant Labor Markets and the Welfare of Rural Households in the Developing World: Evidence from China." Policy Research Working Paper 4585, World Bank, Washington, DC.

Du, Yang, Albert Park, and Sangui Wang. 2005. "Migration and Rural Poverty in China." *Journal of Comparative Economics* 33 (4): 688–709.

Foster, James, Joel Greer, and Eric Thorbecke. 1984. "A Class of Decomposable Poverty Measures." *Econometrica* 52 (3): 761–65.

Giles, John. 2006. "Is Life More Risky in the Open? Household Risk-Coping and the Opening of China's Labor Markets." *Journal of Development Economics* 81 (1): 25–60.

Giles, John, and Ren Mu. 2007. "Elderly Parent Health and the Migration Decision of Adult Children: Evidence from Rural China." *Demography* 44 (2): 265–88.

Giles, John, and Kyeongwon Yoo. 2007. "Precautionary Behavior, Migrant Networks, and Household Consumption Decisions: An Empirical Analysis Using Household Panel Data from Rural China." *Review of Economics and Statistics* 89 (3): 534–51.

Hurd, Michael, and Michael Boskin. 1984. "The Effect of Social Security on Retirement in the Early 1970s." *Quarterly Journal of Economics* 99 (4): 767–90.

Jalan, Jyotsna, and Martin Ravallion. 1999. "Are the Poor Less Well Insured? Evidence on Vulnerability to Income Risk in Rural China." *Journal of Development Economics* 58 (1): 61–81.

Parsons, Donald O. 1980. "The Decline in Male Labor Force Participation." *Journal of Political Economy* 88 (1): 117–34.

CHAPTER 3

Sources of Support among the Rural Elderly

This chapter examines the sources of support among the rural elderly, comparing them with those of the urban elderly and among different sub-cohorts of the rural elderly. It finds that urban and rural elderly show striking differences in their sources of support. Although pension income is the most important source of support for urban households, labor income and family support remain the primary modes of support for the rural elderly. Between the ages of 60 and 70, rural household support shifts from primary reliance on labor income to primary reliance on family support. In light of the aggregate findings, the chapter then looks in more detail at the patterns of family support (including variations between rural elderly households with and without migrant adult children) and examines patterns in the labor supply of the rural elderly.

Sources of Support among China's Elderly

Major differences exist in the primary sources of support for China's urban and rural elderly and between men and women from both groups of elderly. Table 3.1 reports findings on the elderly's sources of support by location and gender for 2005. The differences across groups among the elderly are striking, notably the following:

Table 3.1   Primary Source of Support for China's Elderly, 2005
most significant share of support reported

	Urban			Rural		
Source of support	*Average*	*Male*	*Female*	*Average*	*Male*	*Female*
Labor income	13.0	18.4	7.9	37.9	48.5	27.5
Pensions	45.4	56.9	34.6	4.6	8.1	1.3
Dibao	2.4	1.8	2.9	1.3	1.8	0.9
Insurance and subsidy	0.3	0.3	0.2	0.1	0.2	0.0
Property income	0.5	0.5	0.5	0.2	0.2	0.1
Family support	37.0	20.7	52.3	54.1	39.3	68.5
Other	1.5	1.4	1.6	1.8	2.0	1.7

Source: NBS 2006.

- Although pensions are the single most significant source of support for the urban elderly, they remain a very minor source of support for the rural elderly, almost entirely confined to former civil servants and soldiers, and former village cadres.[1]
- In contrast, labor income is a much more significant source of support for the rural elderly than for the urban elderly, being the primary source of support for 37.9 percent of the rural elderly.
- Family support is an important source of support for both rural and urban elderly households, but its significance among the rural elderly is substantially greater.
- As of 2005, the rural *dibao* was not an important source of income support for rural or urban elderly households.[2] This finding may stem from the fact that the rural *dibao* was still being phased in at the time of the survey, although policy has shifted in the intervening period with the approval of rural *dibao* as national policy in 2007 and a resultant expansion in coverage.[3]
- Also notable is the inability of the elderly to earn income from property. In contrast to member countries of the Organisation for Economic Co-operation and Development historically, or other developing countries today, the elderly in China have not grown old in an environment in which they could accumulate land wealth. Lack of land wealth limits the ability of the elderly to earn income from rents and may also limit the scope for encouraging intergenerational transfers from their children (who would be prospective heirs).

Looking at sources of support by gender among the rural elderly, family support is more important for elderly women and labor income remains more important for men. As shown in table 3.1, 68.5 percent of women over 60 report that financial support from family members is their most important source of support, whereas only 27.5 percent report that labor income is most important. In contrast, 48.5 percent of elderly men report that labor income remains their most important source of support; only 39.3 percent report support from family members. When distinguishing the importance of pension by gender, a significantly higher share of rural men (8.1 percent) than women (1.3 percent) report that pension income is their most significant source of financial support. The gap between men and women reflects historical differences between genders in employment in local government and the military.

Rural elderly in their sixties are more likely to support themselves through labor income, whereas those over 70 depend far more on support from family members. Table 3.2 shows results by age cohort among the rural elderly and emphasizes the differences in financial support between younger and older elderly people. Younger elderly rely more on labor income, and a shift starts after age 70. Notably, however, nearly a quarter of the elderly between 70 and 75 report labor income as their main source of support. Apart from family support and labor income, no other source of support for the elderly varies significantly by age group. Moreover, no other component plays a particularly significant role.

Evidence on Family Support

Until the last few years, policy on pensions and safety nets has not focused significantly on the rural elderly because the family was assumed to be an adequate source of support. Policy makers had assumed the continued

Table 3.2   Source of Support for China's Rural Elderly, by Age Group, 2005
share of income in percent

	Age group (years)						
Source of support	60+	60–64	65–69	70–74	75–79	80–84	85+
Labor income	37.9	64.3	45.1	24.4	12.0	4.3	1.7
Pensions	4.6	4.7	5.1	4.7	4.4	3.8	2.6
Dibao	1.3	0.8	1.2	1.5	1.9	2.0	2.1
Insurance and subsidy	0.1	0.1	0.1	0.1	0.1	0.1	0.1
Property income	0.2	0.1	0.2	0.2	0.2	0.1	0.1
Family support	54.1	28.6	46.6	66.9	79.1	87.2	91.1
Other	1.8	1.2	1.7	2.2	2.3	2.4	2.3

Source: NBS 2006.

viability of traditional, family-based arrangements for two reasons. First, family values remain strong in rural areas, and Confucian filial piety continues to sustain family care for the elderly. Second, any formal public policy response to the needs of the rural elderly may undermine existing private arrangements. For example, state transfers to the elderly may crowd out existing transfers from younger family members.

With regard to the reliance on traditional family values, both policy makers and other observers have in recent years questioned the view that family support for the rural elderly will be sufficient. Fertility decline driven by China's population policies may ultimately lead to a breakdown of the traditional support system, but conclusions from research spanning the literature on demography and economics disagree on the likeliness of this outcome. Zimmer and Kwong (2003) show that more children increase the likelihood that the elderly will receive support, but present simulation results suggest that declines in fertility alone will not lead to a collapse of family-based support for the elderly. Other research has suggested that financial transfers to parents respond to low income and low health status in urban areas (Cai, Giles, and Meng 2006), but that in rural areas interhousehold transfers are not often observed because they take the form of labor input into family farming (Lee and Xiao 1998).[4] The following sections explore some of these questions empirically.

Changes to Living Arrangements and the Well-Being of the Elderly

The share of rural elderly living with their children has declined rapidly, both in the long term and in recent years. Changes in living arrangements have been cited most frequently as reasons for concern for the well-being of the elderly. For example, Benjamin, Brandt, and Rozelle (2000) note that in rural northern China, over 85 percent of the elderly lived in extended households in 1935, but this figure had dropped to just over 60 percent by 1995.[5] The decline in coresidence with adult children is strikingly evident over the six rounds of the China Health and Nutrition Survey (CHNS) from 1991 to 2006. Figure 3.1 shows that in the CHNS, nearly 70 percent of elderly in rural areas lived with an adult child in 1991, but by 2006 this share had fallen to just over 40 percent. As elderly parent age increases, the probability of coresidence with an adult child approaches 100 percent.[6]

At the same time, a decline in coresidence does not necessarily reflect a drop in provision of care to the elderly. In-kind transfers, such as supply

Figure 3.1   Living Arrangements of China's Rural Elderly

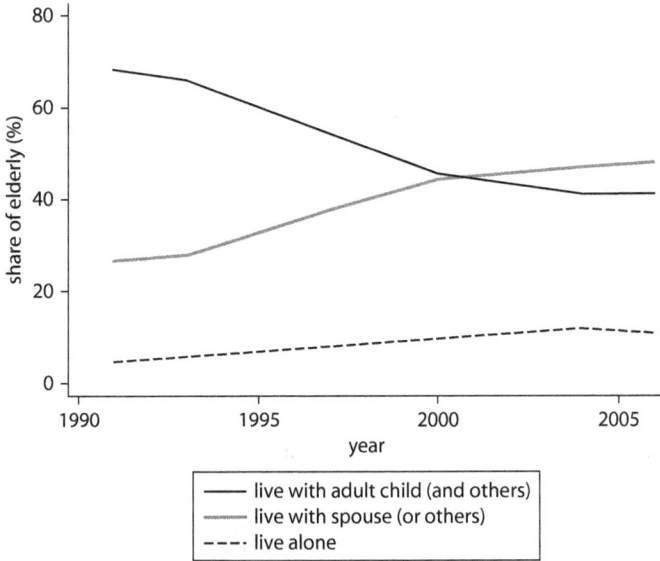

Source: China Health and Nutrition Survey (CHNS), various years.

of labor on extended family plots, are difficult to pick up in surveys, yet such transfers often occur both within and across households. Changes in living arrangements reflect the increasing wealth of families. With increasing resources, coresidence may be unnecessary in caring for the elderly. Within villages in rural areas, elders and adult children are typically in the same small group (a subvillage administrative unit) and live in proximity to one another. Given increases in housing wealth in rural areas since the mid-1980s, the trend toward nuclear families may signal a wealth effect independent of the traditional value of providing support and care to elderly parents.

In addition, the share of rural elderly with an adult child living nearby was actually higher. A more important factor may be the proximity of adult children—and not whether they coreside. Figure 3.2 summarizes the living arrangements by age cohort from the 2004 Research Center for Rural Economy (RCRE) supplemental survey and includes information on children living within the same village as their elders. Although coresidence with adult children was less than 60 percent during the 2003 reference period among those 60 to 70 years of age, more than half the elderly living alone or with a spouse in this age range had at least one

Figure 3.2   Living Arrangements of China's Rural Elderly, by Age

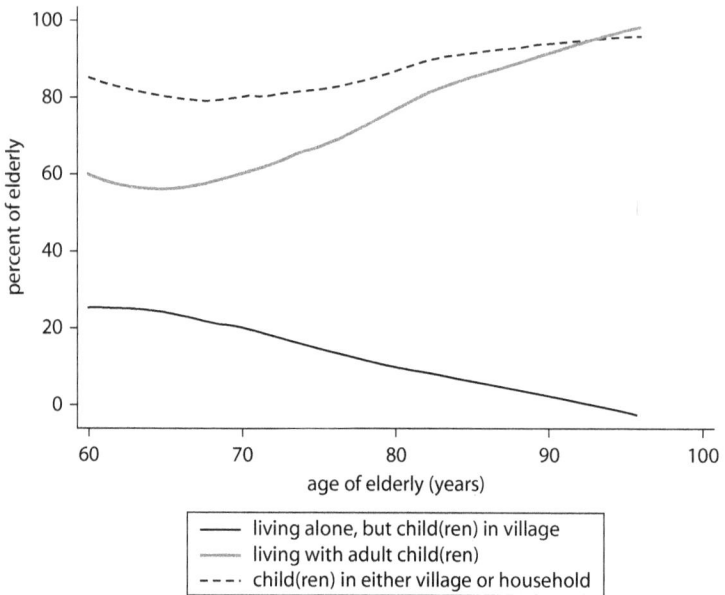

Source: RCRE 2004.

adult child living in the village.[7] This finding suggests that even though coresidence was well below the levels of the 1930s, adult children were still potentially available to provide care.

Evidence suggests that migration decisions of adult children are influenced by the well-being of elderly parents. Decline in coresidence reflects a decline in support for the elderly only if it is associated with increased abandonment of the elderly. The rural elderly may have sufficient support if they are receiving transfers from local or migrant adult children. Giles and Mu (2007) explore this possibility by conducting separate analyses using two different data sources. They find a significantly lower probability that a son will work as a migrant when a parent is seriously ill. Although parental illness has a statistically significant effect on migration, it does not completely drive the decision to return from migrant destinations. Depending on the data set and methodology, the effect of illness varied from a 15 percent to 26 percent reduction in the probability that a son would be employed as a migrant, and this effect was reduced if other siblings remained behind in the village. Although this level of responsiveness to elderly illness is significant, it is not absolute. Moreover, elderly who are relatively healthy may have a much lower standard of living if nonresident adult children who are migrants are less likely to make transfers to their parents than adult children who live nearby. In light of these findings, the next section examines how private transfers respond to low income of the elderly, including whether transfer responsiveness differs with migrant children.

Do Private Transfers Respond to Income of the Elderly?

Two important reasons exist to examine the responsiveness of transfers and transfer levels. First, as China rolls out its national rural pension program, concerns may arise about formal support for the elderly crowding out transfers from private sources. Second, although the findings in chapter 2 suggest that elderly households with migrant family members may be less likely to fall into poverty, those findings are average effects and do not explore how transfers vary with pretransfer household income, nor do they consider the distribution of transfers and the risks that the elderly may fall into poverty if transfers do not materialize.

Much early research on intrafamily transfers used data from developed countries and focused on efforts to distinguish whether transfers were motivated by altruistic or exchange motives.[8] This distinction is important because it has implications for how transfers respond to income received by elderly households. If an altruistic motive dominates, family members outside the household may respond to reduced levels of income by providing an offsetting transfer. This possibility may mean that any increase in income—a pension payment, for example—would lead to an offsetting reduction in private transfers into the household. If the altruistic motive dominates, private transfers to elderly family members will likely fall as public transfers increase (private transfers are "crowded out"). In contrast, when exchange motives or other motives are more important, one is unlikely to observe a significant reduction in such private transfers and crowding out is less of a concern.

This section shows that (a) the risk of private transfers being insufficient to prevent elderly poverty has increased in recent years and (b) public transfers (for example, pensions or *dibao*) are unlikely to crowd out private transfers to the rural elderly even at very low levels of income. Thus, the receipt of pensions or targeted public transfers would likely improve the welfare of the rural elderly. Moreover, when transfer behavior from an early period (1995–99) is compared with that of a later period (2000–03), a notable increase is seen in the risk that transfers to low-income elderly will be insufficient to prevent them from falling into poverty.[9] Second, although migrants respond to their elderly parents' low income by transferring more income, the wide confidence interval in predicted levels of transfers implies that some elderly are at risk of falling into poverty.

Private transfers respond to low pretransfer income regardless of the migrant status of adult children. Figure 3.3 shows that transfers from family members decline in response to increases in the income level of the elderly household. It also shows how transfers respond to pretransfer income levels for elderly households that have migrant children and those that do not. To highlight changes in transfer responsiveness over time, the results are shown separately for the periods 1995–98 and 2000–03. The key findings are as follows:

- For both periods and for households with and without migrant adult children, net transfers fall sharply as rural elderly household income rises. The findings suggest that private transfers continue to respond to the low income of elderly parents regardless of migrant status.
- For the period 1995–98, transfers to elderly households were more responsive to income at low levels if the elderly had migrant children than if they did not. This finding suggests that, in this earlier period, public transfers to the elderly with migrant children would have crowded out more private transfers at very low levels of income. However, at income levels near the poverty line, the transfer derivative was −0.5 for elderly households regardless of whether they had migrant children. Thus, even in the 1990s, one would not expect private transfers to be crowded out completely by payments from a public transfer in elderly households already at or above the poverty line.
- By 2000–03, private net transfers into households with elderly members were less responsive to income for households with migrant children. This decline in transfer responsiveness holds for the significant share of households with incomes ranging from half the poverty line to twice that value. It also indicates that concerns about public transfers crowding out private transfers are becoming less relevant over time. Indeed, the decline in responsiveness of transfers to low income raises the possibility that the elderly may be more exposed to the risk of poverty with increases in out-migration of adult children and the increasing likelihood that migration of children is permanent.

Figure 3.3   Net Transfers Received by Rural Elderly, by Migrant Status of Adult Children

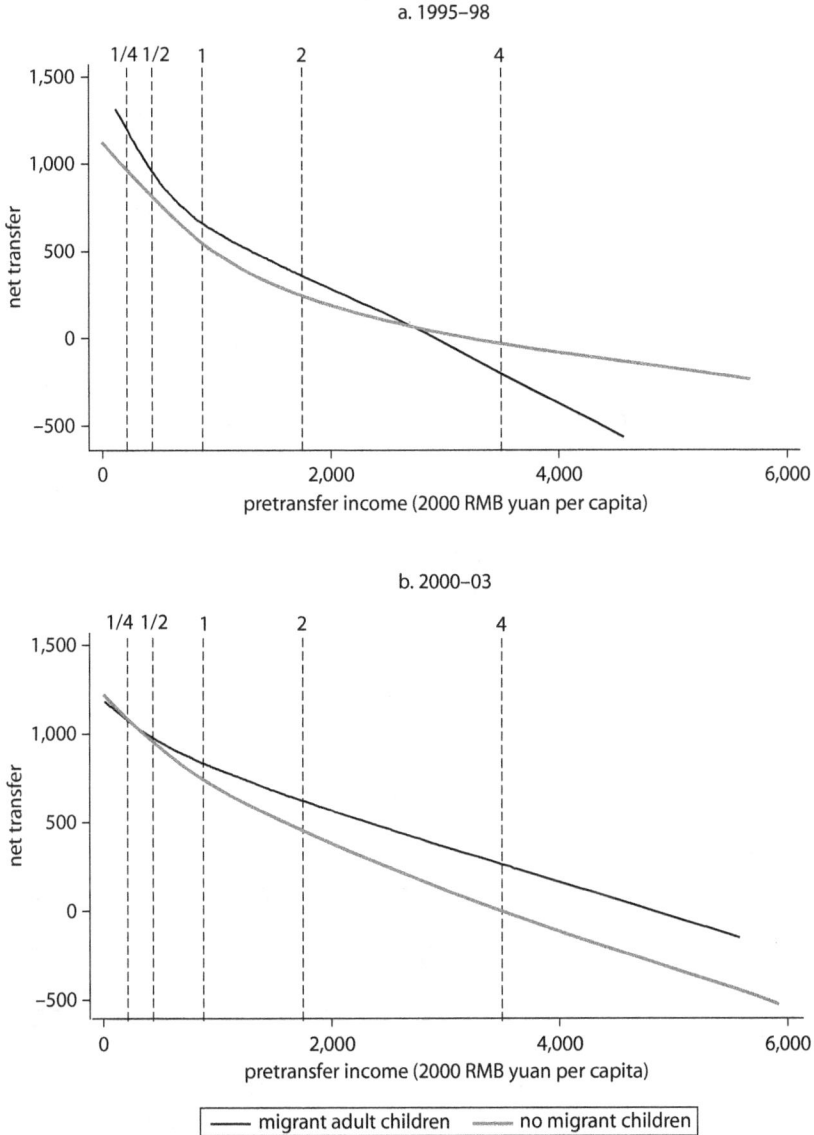

a. 1995–98

b. 2000–03

migrant adult children ——— no migrant children

Sources: Giles, Wang, and Zhao 2010, estimated using data from RCRE Rural Household Surveys for 1995–2003 from Anhui, Henan, Jiangsu, and Shanxi provinces and the matched RCRE 2004.
Note: Vertical lines indicate multiples of a nutrition-based poverty line, which is equal to 875 RMB yuan per capita in 2000 RMB.

To highlight how transfers respond to income at different points in the income distribution, table 3.3 reports the transfer response at different multiples of the poverty line. As the table shows, the likelihood of transfers falls notably in both periods for elderly households with and without migrant children as the income of the elderly household increases.

Thus, during the period 1995–98, elderly households with migrant family members appear very unlikely to have income per capita below the poverty line after private transfers are included in household income. To assess the risk that private transfers are insufficient to keep the elderly out of poverty, figure 3.4 shows that the combinations of pretransfer income and private transfers are sufficient to keep elderly households above the poverty threshold. That threshold is represented in figure 3.4 as the straight line running from the y-axis when pretransfer income is zero to the point on the x-axis where net transfers are −500 renminbi (RMB) per capita and the household pretransfer income is just enough to keep the household out of poverty. Panels a and b of figure 3.4 show the predicted range of net transfers for different levels of pretransfer income from 1995 to 1998 for households without and with migrants, respectively. Comparing those two figures, more of the lower bound of transfers lies below the poverty threshold for households without migrant family members.

After 2000, elderly households with migrant family members are at greater risk of falling into poverty. From panels c and d of figure 3.4, one can clearly see that households with incomes of less than half the poverty line are more at risk, for which transfers will be insufficient to raise total income above the poverty line. The lower responsiveness of transfers to

Table 3.3   Estimated Transfer Derivatives for Households with Elderly Residents
estimates in neighborhood of multiple of the poverty line

Multiple	Income per capita (RMB)	Households without migrant children		Households with migrant children	
		1996–98	2000–03	1996–98	2000–03
One-quarter poverty line	119 to 319	−0.84	−0.67	−1.73	−0.63
One-half poverty line	338 to 538	−0.73	−0.57	−1.03	−0.35
Poverty line	775 to 975	−0.52	−0.46	−0.49	−0.25
Twice poverty line	1,650 to 1,850	−0.28	−0.35	−0.40	−0.21
Four times poverty line	3,400 to 3,600	−0.11	−0.24	−0.31	−0.20

Sources: Giles, Wang, and Zhao 2010, estimates based on RCRE Rural Household Surveys for 1995–2003 from Anhui, Henan, Jiangsu, and Shanxi provinces and the matched RCRE 2004.
Note: All values are in 2000 RMB yuan per capita. The nutrition-based poverty line is equal to 875 RMB yuan per capita.

Figure 3.4 Confidence Intervals for Net Transfers Received by Rural Elderly, by Migrant Status of Adult Children

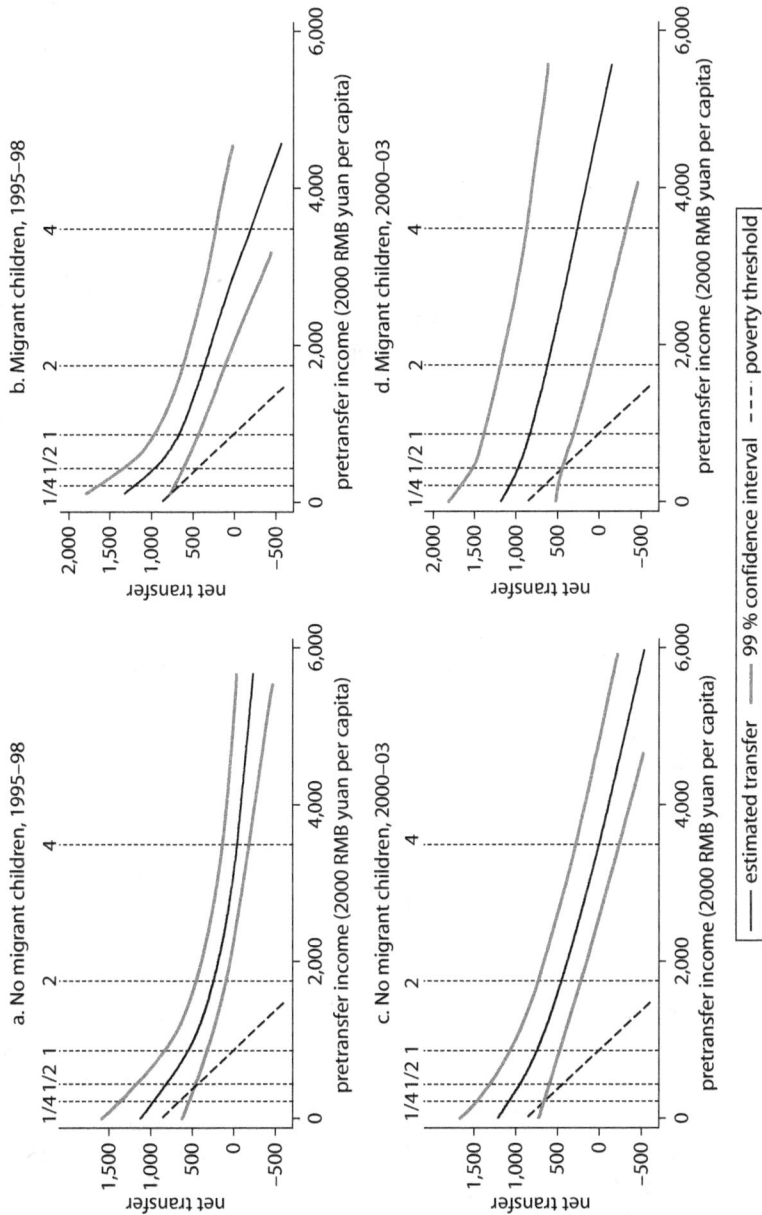

a. No migrant children, 1995–98

b. Migrant children, 1995–98

c. No migrant children, 2000–03

d. Migrant children, 2000–03

estimated transfer   99 % confidence interval   - - - poverty threshold

Sources: Giles, Wang, and Zhao 2010, estimated using data from RCRE Rural Household Surveys for 1995–2003 from Anhui, Henan, Jiangsu, and Shanxi provinces and the matched RCRE 2004.

Note: Vertical lines indicate multiples of a nutrition-based poverty line, which is equal to 875 RMB yuan per capita in 2000 RMB.

low incomes suggests that a noncontributory pension or other support mechanism is unlikely to crowd out private transfers.

Evidence summarized in table 3.4 also suggests that elderly households with pretransfer income per capita below one-half the nutrition-based poverty line are at particular risk of falling into poverty. Table 3.4 summarizes the range of transfers at five multiples of the poverty line.

When considering the results from the four-province analysis of transfers, one should remember that although poorer areas of Anhui, Shanxi, and Henan are included in the analysis sample, these provinces are generally considered middle income, and Jiangsu is included among upper-income coastal provinces. If transfer responsiveness to low income is also declining among households with migrant children in poorer regions of China, then a higher share of elderly households are likely to be at risk of slipping into poverty.

The Labor Supply and "Retirement" Decision of China's Rural Elderly

Recent studies of retirement decisions in rural China suggest that rural elderly "work until they drop" and stop working only when they are physically incapacitated (Pang, de Brauw, and Rozelle 2004). Benjamin, Brandt, and Fan (2003) find evidence suggesting that the likelihood of working in agriculture declines significantly with increases in family wealth, raising the possibility that public transfers might facilitate reduced labor supply of the rural elderly. In China's urban areas, where many of the elderly rely on pension support, relatively few elderly continue to work in retirement. In contrast, the discussion earlier noted that nearly 50 percent of rural men and 28 percent of women over retirement age state that income from work remains their primary source of support. Because a considerable number of elderly receiving family support also continue to work, these figures significantly understate the degree to which China's rural elderly continue to work after retirement age.

Even as family wealth and incomes have increased among households in rural China, in recent years China's rural elderly were more likely to work. Employment rates increase at every age for elderly relatives of RCRE panel households over the period from 1993 to 2003 (see figure 3.5).[10] In fact, continued employment of the elderly may be an important contributing factor to the rising incomes of rural households. As rural household incomes increase with the migrant employment of

Table 3.4 Estimated Range of Transfers to Households with Elderly Residents, Results for Neighborhoods of Different Multiples of the Poverty Line

Multiple	Pretransfer income per capita	Portion of estimated range	1995–98 Households without migrant children	1995–98 Households with migrant children	2000–03 Households without migrant children	2000–03 Households with migrant children
One-quarter poverty line	119 to 319	Upper bound	1,356	1,643	1,489	1,655
		Mean	948	1,216	1,081	1,071
		Lower bound	531	718	664	479
One-half poverty line	338 to 538	Upper bound	1,155	1,276	1,293	1,484
		Mean	811	910	942	953
		Lower bound	469	610	601	461
Poverty line	775 to 975	Upper bound	785	908	1,019	1,381
		Mean	517	648	709	821
		Lower bound	307	420	473	290
Two times poverty line	1,650 to 1,850	Upper bound	421	605	701	1192
		Mean	212	369	433	615
		Lower bound	87	120	216	55
Four times poverty line	3,400 to 3,600	Upper bound	125	216	259	862
		Mean	–48	–137	–7	274
		Lower bound	–185	–568	–249	–345

Sources: Giles, Wang, and Zhao 2010, estimates based on RCRE Rural Household Surveys for 1995–2003 from Anhui, Henan, Jiangsu, and Shanxi provinces and the matched RCRE 2004.
Note: All values are in 2000 RMB yuan per capita. The nutrition-based poverty line is equal to 875 RMB yuan per capita.

Figure 3.5   Employment Status of the Rural Elderly over Time

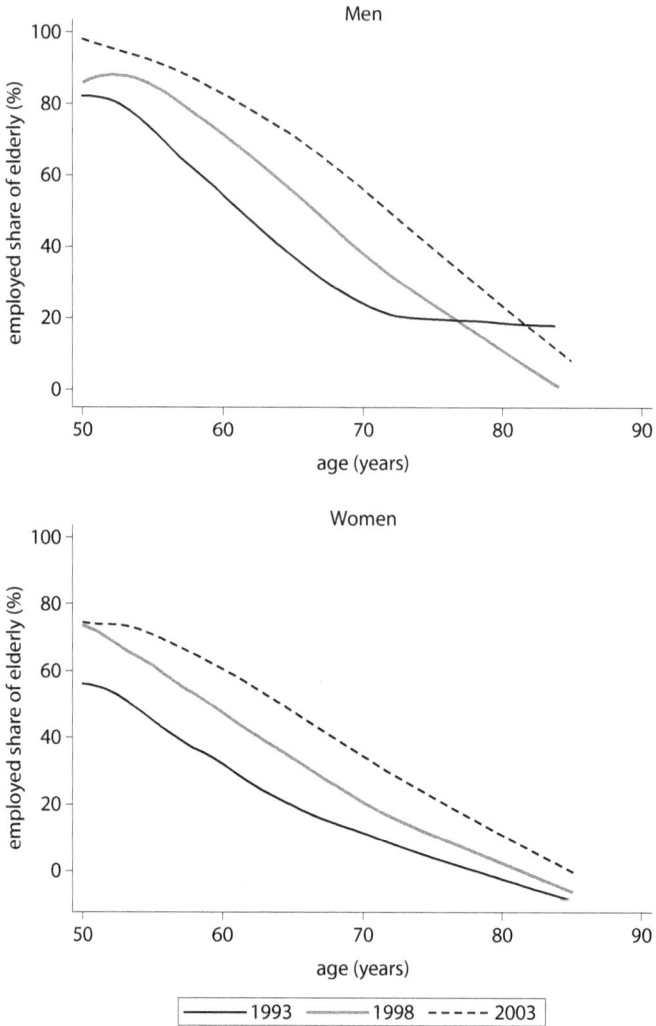

Source: Cai, Giles, and Wang 2009, using survey data from RCRE 2004.

younger adults, older parents remain behind and continue farming the household land.

Features of China's land tenure system may contribute to the effect of child migration on the labor supply of the elderly. Access to land in rural China has long been the safety net for able-bodied rural residents, but restrictions on the ability to transfer land may also influence labor supply decisions. The inability to rent land further reduces the income of an elderly person in retirement, and the possibility that village leaders will reallocate land that is not kept productive may create additional incentives for older farmers to continue working household land. Changes in the Land Law enacted in 2002 and 2003 may have facilitated land transfer and presumably may also have influenced the labor supply decisions of older rural residents.

No systematic relationship between elderly retirement and migration status of children is immediately evident. To examine the possibility that migration of children is systematically related to labor supply decisions of the elderly, figure 3.6 shows the share of age cohorts employed by migrant status for men and women in 1998 and 2003. At the same time, however, migration status of children and the labor supply decision of an elderly household resident are both systematically related to household composition, family wealth, earning ability of family members, and health status of the elderly person in question. To better characterize the relationship between (a) migration and (b) retirement and labor supply decisions of the elderly, it is important to explicitly model the labor supply decision of the elderly while controlling for these other factors.

The employment status and location of adult children may have an important effect on the retirement decision. However, the likely effect of a migrant child is ambiguous. On one hand, a migrant adult child may raise household income through increased remittances more than the migrant lowers income through lack of work in agriculture. In this case, one would expect the existence of a migrant son or daughter to be negatively associated with elderly parent labor supply. On the other hand, if loss of work capacity when a child migrates is not offset by remittances, migration of an adult child may make an elderly parent's retirement more difficult. Moreover, if residents of a village lose land when it is not kept productive, land tenure insecurity may create an additional disincentive for retirement.

This analysis finds notable variation by gender differences according to whether the individual is among the younger or older elderly. Coefficient estimates from labor supply models of participation and hours worked in productive activity are shown in tables 3.5 and 3.6, respectively. Labor supply of the elderly is affected by the following factors:

- *Increases in actual (or potential) household income from other sources reduce the likelihood of an older person still working.* This factor is evident

Figure 3.6 Correlation of Employment of Elderly and Migrant Status of Adult Children

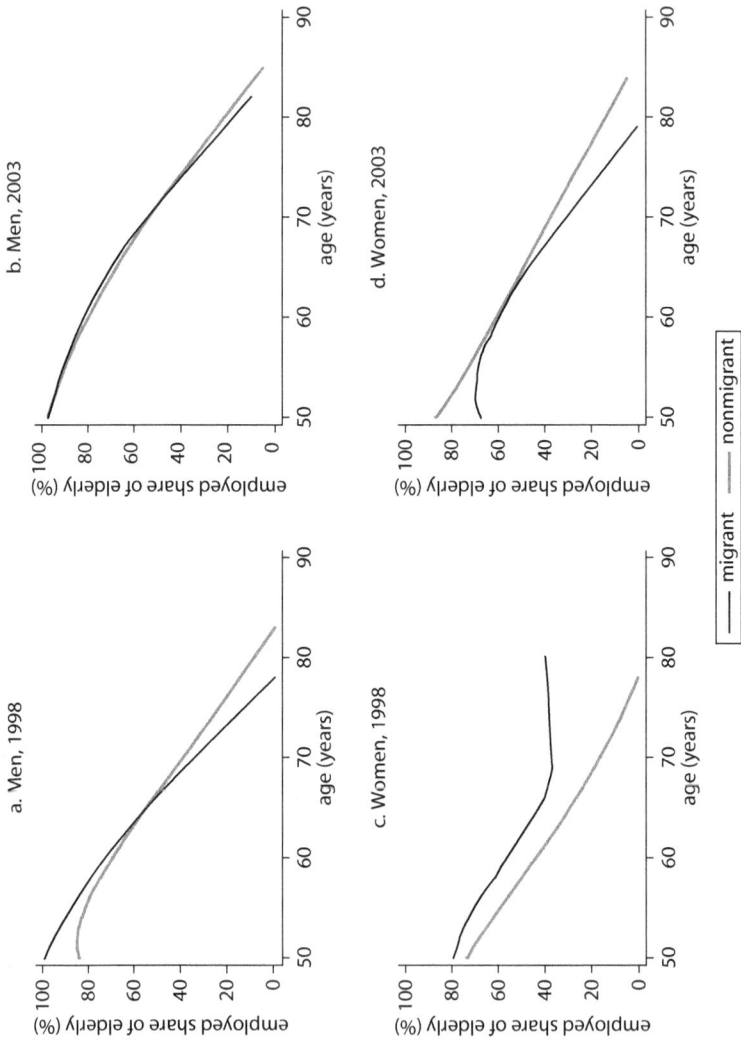

a. Men, 1998

b. Men, 2003

c. Women, 1998

d. Women, 2003

migrant — nonmigrant

Source: Cai, Giles, and Wang 2009, estimated using RCRE 2004.

in table 3.5 from examining the effects of pension receipt and educational attainment on employment. For each 1,000 RMB per capita received as pension income, the probability that a man works (whether in his sixties or seventies) falls by 8 percent, and the probability that a woman works falls by about 6 percent. Educational attainment of men in their sixties has no significant effect on employment, but each additional year of education is associated with a 1.6 percent reduction in the probability that a woman in her sixties is employed, and a 1.2 percent to 1.3 percent reduction in the probability that elderly in their seventies are working. An increase in the average years of education of other family members has an even stronger depressing effect on labor force participation: higher average levels of education are associated with higher permanent income of the family, which facilitates retirement.

- *Ill health, as represented by increases in the activity of daily living (ADL) z-score,[11] also lowers the likelihood that an individual engages in productive activities.* Because men are often tasked with more

Table 3.5 Factors Affecting Labor Supply Decisions of the Elderly, Linear Model
dependent variable: engaged in productive activities during the year

| | Ages 60–70 | | Ages 70–80 | |
Variable	Men	Women	Men	Women
Has migrant member	0.009	0.058	0.010	0.081***
	(0.041)	(0.046)	(0.046)	(0.032)
Years of education	−0.005	−0.016***	−0.013***	−0.012**
	(0.004)	(0.005)	(0.004)	(0.006)
Years of education of other household members	−0.017***	−0.020***	−0.018***	−0.015***
	(0.005)	(0.005)	(0.005)	(0.004)
ADL z-score	−0.113***	−0.079***	−0.103***	−0.049**
	(0.029)	(0.026)	(0.022)	(0.020)
Income from pension/1,000 RMB	−0.083***	−0.064***	−0.084***	−0.060***
	(0.012)	(0.012)	(0.011)	(0.010)
R-squared	0.237	0.287	0.261	0.179
Observations	483	586	705	818

Sources: CHNS 1991, 1993, 1997, 2000, and 2004.
Note: Migrant family member = a member of the household from a previous round is no longer a household member and has moved outside the home province.
All models include age, age-squared, household demographic variables (number of household members over 60, number of children younger than 3, children 3–7, children 8–13, children 14–16, spouse present), and year dummy variables interacted with regions to control for provincewide macroeconomic effects.
Standard errors are shown in parentheses.
*, **, *** indicate significance at 10, 5, and 1 percent, respectively.

physically demanding jobs in agriculture, this effect is, not surprisingly, stronger for men in both age categories than for women. A one standard deviation increase in the ADL z-score is associated with 11.3 percent and 7.9 percent decreases in probability of employment for men and women, respectively, in their sixties, and a 10.3 percent and 4.9 percent decrease, respectively, for men and women in their seventies.

- *Migration of adult children is weakly associated with increased labor supply*. A positive association exists between a migrant child and increased labor supply, but it is not statistically significant for men or for women under 70. Lost farm income and uncertainty about land tenure likely dominate the effects of increased income from remittances when the elderly make decisions about working. Women over 70, however, are 8.1 percent more likely to continue working (most likely in agriculture) if the household has a migrant child.

Evidence on hours worked, presented in table 3.6, suggests that migrant adult children have the strongest effect on the work behavior of women over age 70. Women over 70 with a migrant child work 411 hours more during a year, or the equivalent of 10 40-hour workweeks. For regions of the country that plant two crops a year, that would amount to full-time work during the agricultural busy season. The effects of education on hours worked are of the same direction as in the employment models of table 3.5, but once employed, education itself does not strongly affect the number of hours worked.

As might be expected, the number of hours worked by the rural elderly is also very sensitive to their health status and to income from pensions. An increase in one standard deviation of the ADL index is associated with a 417-hour reduction in hours worked by men in their sixties, and a reduction of 294 hours by men in their seventies. Women in their sixties reduce labor supply by 300 hours with a one standard deviation increase in their ADL index, whereas women in their seventies reduce labor supply by 212 hours in response to a similar worsening in their health. Pension income also has a stronger depressing effect on hours worked by men in their sixties.

The urban elderly are much less likely to work after 60 than are the rural elderly. And the results presented here suggest that any mechanism providing the rural elderly with an income flow in old age will likely reduce both employment and hours worked. As China's government rolls

Table 3.6   Factors Affecting Hours Worked by the Elderly, Tobit Model
dependent variable: hours worked

Variable	Ages 60–70		Ages 70–80	
	Men	*Women*	*Men*	*Women*
Has migrant child	44.3	−7.6	199.1	411.2**
	(168.6)	(146.3)	(162.1)	(162.7)
Years of education	15.2	−1.5	−27.0*	−14.3
	(18.3)	(16.1)	(15.1)	(21.5)
Education of other	−12.3	−53.1***	−40.4**	−45.5***
household members	(19.6)	(16.6)	(18.8)	(16.0)
ADL z-score	−416.9***	−299.9***	−294.4***	−211.6***
	(132.7)	(94.8)	(85.1)	(70.6)
Income from	−447.9***	−314.1***	−350.4***	−308.0***
pension/1,000 RMB	(71.1)	(56.7)	(52.9)	(49.0)
Observations	479	586	705	816

Sources: CHNS 1991, 1993, 1997, 2000 and 2004.
Note: Migrant family member = a member of the household from a previous round is no longer a household member and has moved outside the home province.
All models include age, age-squared, household demographic variables (number of household members over 60, number of children younger than 3, children 3–7, children 8–13, children 14–16, spouse present), and year dummy variables interacted with regions to control for province-wide macroeconomic effects.
Standard errors are shown in parentheses.
*, **, *** indicate significance at 10, 5, and 1 percent, respectively.

out a national pension system for the rural elderly, rural residents will likely choose to "retire" rather than work until they are no longer able to do so, depending of course on the benefit level.

Conclusion

Whereas the urban elderly receive significant support from pensions, the rural elderly rely primarily on their own labor income and financial support from their children. More men over 60 rely primarily on their own labor income for support, whereas elderly women are somewhat more dependent on transfers from family members. Evidence presented on responsiveness of private transfers to income levels and on the determinants of elderly labor supply suggests that the introduction of a pension system may lead to more security for the elderly without requiring them to continue working into old age.

Private transfers are responsive to low levels of elderly income, but they do not perfectly crowd out income from other sources. At levels of income below the poverty line, transfers from adult children increase as elderly income decreases. When elderly incomes are at and even below the poverty line, however, private transfers are not perfectly crowded out by increases in income. A social welfare benefit that raises incomes of the elderly will not crowd out private transfers.

Migrant children continue to provide remittance support to their parents, but the predicted range of transfers suggests growing risk that low-income elderly may be left in poverty. On average, the predicted transfer from adult children is sufficient to maintain elderly incomes above the poverty line. When the range of potential transfers is considered, however, elderly with migrant children clearly face more risk that private transfers will be insufficient to maintain standards of living above the poverty line.

Elderly with higher incomes are less likely to work, as are elderly who are in poor health. Elderly with nonlabor income from pensions or in households with higher levels of education, and thus more income-earning potential, are less likely to participate in income-earning activities. If the elderly receive some type of social welfare support, they are more likely to exit the labor force when they are over 60.

Elderly in poor health are less likely to work. Declines in health status associated with decreases in ability to perform daily tasks are associated with lower participation in work activity and fewer working hours for those who are still working. Improving use of the health care system for preventive purposes may keep older workers productive and earning incomes for a longer period of their lives. Further research examining the effects of the New Cooperative Medical System is warranted to determine whether it facilitates improved health and work capacity of older workers.

Migration of adult children may significantly affect the work status of elderly women. Having a migrant child in the family raises the probability that a woman over 70 will still be in the labor force and, conditional on working, will work more hours in a year. For men and women under 70, a migrant child has a positive but statistically insignificant effect on participation in income-earning activities.

Notes

1. The data were collected before initiation of the national rural pension pilot program in 2009.
2. This finding is consistent with findings in the World Bank's China poverty assessment (Chaudhuri and Datt 2009) using other National Bureau of Statistics data.

3. See World Bank (forthcoming) for a detailed discussion of the evolution of rural *dibao* and other forms of rural social assistance, noting coverage expansion of rural *dibao* from just over 8 million in 2005 to almost 48 million in 2009.

4. Using other methods, Cameron and Cobb-Clark (2008) find no evidence that transfers to parents respond to low parent income in Indonesia.

5. Selden (1993) concludes that a transition to the nuclear family imposes a heavy price on the rural elderly. Living arrangements are thought to be important for elderly support across East Asia, including Cambodia (Zimmer and Kim 2002), Thailand (Knodel and Chayovan 1997), and Vietnam (Anh and others 1997).

6. Two very different conclusions are consistent with evidence of greater incidence of coresidence with age: the oldest, who are more likely to be infirm, tend to move in with adult children; alternatively, if coresidence has an effect on the quality of care provided, then perhaps only the elderly living with adult children reach old age.

7. Coresidence in rural areas of the four RCRE provinces was also somewhat higher than that observed for rural areas of the CHNS panel.

8. Barro (1974), Becker (1974), and Cox (1987) make important distinctions highlighting different motives for transfers. Much of the empirical research in the United States has suggested that intergenerational inter vivos transfers are driven by exchange motives (for example, Cox and Rank 1992; McGarry 1999) rather than by altruistic motives. However, in the United States, the social security safety net provides substantial insurance against poverty in old age, and thus it is not surprising to find an emphasis on the flow of resources from older to younger generations.

9. Knowing whether a household has family members who have migrated is important for making comparisons across households with migrant children and those with family members living locally. The most appropriate existing data source for the study of transfer behavior is the RCRE household survey, complemented by a supplemental survey conducted in RCRE households in 2004. This book uses the 1995 to 2003 waves of RCRE's annual household survey from four provinces (Anhui, Henan, Jiangsu, and Shanxi) in which a supplemental survey (*Supplemental Rural Household Social Network, Labor Allocation, and Land Use Survey*) was carried out in collaboration with Michigan State University in 2004. A description of the RCRE survey and a comparison with other household surveys in China can be found in Benjamin, Brandt, and Giles (2005). An important feature of the survey is that it enumerated characteristics of former household members, including their current location and educational attainment. Among the factors influencing the size of private transfers, the analysis includes the number of children (which captures the effect of the potential transfer network size on

which rural elderly can rely for private transfers) and average education of children living outside the household (which proxies for the quality of the network). Other regressors included in the analysis are age, years of schooling, marital status, whether any household members are in school, number of household residents, number of working household residents, shares of household residents in different demographic categories, numbers of non-resident family members in different demographic categories, village variables to control for the local economic environment, and province-year variables to control for macroeconomic shocks. The analysis uses the approach introduced by Yatchew (2003) and implemented for analysis of transfers in China by Cai, Giles, and Meng (2006).

10. The information comes from a retrospective work history carried out as part of a supplemental survey conducted with RCRE in 2004. The supplemental survey asked about the work history of current and former household residents and their parents.

11. In the CHNS, activities of daily living (ADLs) are captured by questions asking individuals over age 50 to rate the difficulty from 1 (no difficulty) to 4 (cannot do at all) of the following activities: walking a kilometer; sitting continuously for two hours; standing up after sitting for a long time; climbing one staircase; lifting or raising a 5 kg bag; squatting down, kneeling down or bending over; bathing yourself; eating by yourself; putting on your clothes; and using the toilet. Average responses are calculated for male and female elderly, and then z-scores are calculated for each individual.

References

Anh, Truong, Bui T. Cuong, Daniel Goodkind, and John Knodel. 1997. "Living Arrangements, Patrilinearity and Sources of Support among Elderly Vietnamese." *Asia-Pacific Population Journal* 12 (4): 69–88.

Barro, Robert J. 1974. "Are Government Bonds Net Wealth?" *Journal of Political Economy* 82 (6): 1095–1117.

Becker, Gary. 1974. "A Theory of Social Interactions." *Journal of Political Economy* 82 (6): 1063–93.

Benjamin, Dwayne, Loren Brandt, and Jia-Zhueng Fan. 2003. "Ceaseless Toil? Health and Labor Supply of the Elderly in Rural China." William Davidson Institute Working Paper 579, Department of Economics, University of Toronto, Canada.

Benjamin, Dwayne, Loren Brandt, and John Giles. 2005. "The Evolution of Income Inequality in Rural China." *Economic Development and Cultural Change* 53 (4): 769–824.

Benjamin, Dwayne, Loren Brandt, and Scott Rozelle. 2000. "Aging, Well-Being, and Social Security in Rural North China." *Population and Development Review* 26 (suppl.): 89–116.

Cai, Fang, John Giles, and Xin Meng. 2006. "How Well Do Children Insure Parents against Low Retirement Income? An Analysis Using Survey Data from Urban China." *Journal of Public Economics* 90 (12): 2229–55.

Cai, Fang, John Giles, and Dewen Wang. 2009. "The Well-Being of China's Rural Elderly." Background Paper for East Asia Social Protection Team, World Bank, Washington, DC.

Cameron, Lisa, and Deborah Cobb-Clark. 2008. "Do Coresidency and Financial Transfers from Children Reduce the Need for Elderly Parents to Work in Developing Countries?" *Journal of Population Economics* 21 (4): 1007–33.

CHNS (China Health and Nutrition Survey). Various years. China Center for Disease Control and Prevention and the Carolina Population Center, University of North Carolina at Chapel Hill. http://www.cpc.unc.edu/projects/china.

Chaudhuri, Shubham, and Gaurav Datt. 2009. *From Poor Areas to Poor People: China's Evolving Poverty Agenda, an Assessment of Poverty and Inequality in China*. Washington, DC: World Bank.

Cox, Donald. 1987. "Motives for Private Income Transfers." *Journal of Political Economy* 95 (3): 509–46.

Cox, Donald, and Mark R. Rank. 1992. "Inter-Vivos Transfers and Intergenerational Exchange." *Review of Economics and Statistics* 74 (2): 305–14.

Giles, John, and Ren Mu. 2007. "Elderly Parent Health and the Migration Decision of Adult Children: Evidence from Rural China." *Demography* 44 (2): 265–88.

Giles, John, Dewen Wang, and Changbao Zhao. 2010. "Can China's Rural Elderly Count on Support from Adult Children? Implications of Rural-to-Urban Migration." *Journal of Population Ageing* 3 (3–4): 183–204.

Knodel, John, and Napaporn Chayovan. 1997. "Family Support and Living Arrangements of Thai Elderly." *Asia-Pacific Population Journal* 12 (4): 51–68.

Lee, Yean-Ju, and Zhenyu Xiao. 1998. "Children's Support for Elderly Parents in Urban and Rural China: Results from a National Survey." *Journal of Cross-Cultural Gerontology* 13 (1): 39–62.

McGarry, Kathleen. 1999. "Inter-Vivos Transfers and Intended Bequests." *Journal of Public Economics* 73 (3): 321–25.

NBS (National Bureau of Statistics). 2006. *2005 One Percent Population Sample Data*. Beijing: China Statistics Press.

Pang, Lihua, Alan de Brauw, and Scott Rozelle. 2004. "Working until You Drop: The Elderly of Rural China." *China Journal* 52: 73–96.

RCRE (Research Center for Rural Economy). Various years. *Rural Household Surveys* for 1993–2003 from Anhui, Henan, Jiangsu, and Shanxi Provinces. Beijing: Ministry of Agriculture, Research Center for the Rural Economy.

———. 2004. *Supplemental Rural Household Social Network, Labor Allocation, and Land Use Survey.* Beijing: Ministry of Agriculture, Research Center for the Rural Economy.

Selden, Mark. 1993. "Family Strategies and Structures in Rural North China." In *Chinese Families in the Post-Mao Era*, ed. D. Davis and S. Harrell, 139–64. Berkeley: University of California Press.

World Bank. Forthcoming. *Social Assistance in Rural China: Tackling Poverty through Rural Dibao.* Washington, DC: World Bank.

Yatchew, Adonis. 2003. *Semiparametric Regression for the Applied Econometrician.* Cambridge: Cambridge University Press.

Zimmer, Zachary, and Sovan Kiry Kim. 2002. "Living Arrangements and Socio-Demographic Conditions of Older Adults in Cambodia." Policy Research Division Working Paper 157, Population Council, New York, NY.

Zimmer, Zachary, and Julia Kwong. 2003. "Family Size and Support of Older Adults in Urban and Rural China: Current Effects and Future Implications." *Demography* 40 (1): 23–44.

CHAPTER 4

Saving Decisions in Rural China

This chapter examines the saving behavior of both working-age rural adults and the rural elderly. It first discusses China's high saving rates and then reviews (a) descriptive evidence on saving behavior with an eye toward possible explanations for saving decisions and (b) differences in saving behavior of households with and without migrant family members and households with and without social security. The chapter finds that saving-rate patterns of rural households differ significantly over the age distribution, by migration status of family members and by social security coverage. Rural households without elderly members have higher saving rates; those with migrant members have higher saving rates than those without. As might be expected, saving rates decline with age after 55, but average saving rates always remain positive, even into advanced old age. Little comparable decline occurs in saving rates in elderly households with migrants, which likely reflects the perceived transitory nature of remittance income. The difference in saving behavior between rural households with and without social security benefits, however, is significant and consistent over time.

Why Is the Household Saving Rate So High in China?

The household saving rate in China has been increasing since the reform era started in 1978, although it has been more volatile over time in rural areas than in urban areas. Figure 4.1 shows the trends in household saving rates for rural and urban China over the reform period. From 1978 to 2008, the rural household saving rate was higher in most years than the urban rate, rising from 13.1 percent to 23.1 percent over the period and peaking at 28.6 percent in 1999. Reflecting the greater variability of income in rural areas, one also observes more volatility around the trend of the rural saving rate than for urban households. In the early reform period, the rural saving rate rose to 22.9 percent in 1984 after successful implementation of the household responsibility system, but it dropped sharply during the inflationary years of the late 1980s and the subsequent slowdown during the early 1990s. The saving rate again trended upward

Figure 4.1   Trends of Household Saving Rates in Rural and Urban China

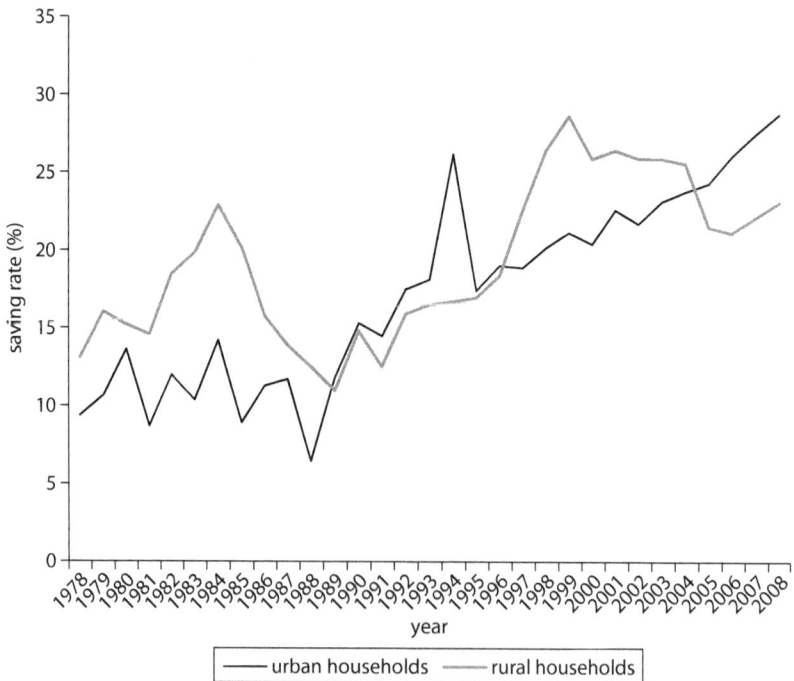

Sources: NBS 2005a, 2009.
Note: Savings = disposable income (or net income) – consumption expenditure.

between 1995 and 1999, then leveled off at over 25 percent for the following four years before dropping from 2003 to 2006. The urban saving rate has fluctuated less around a consistent upward trend since the early 1990s and in recent years has been higher than the rural saving rate. The effect of the global financial crisis on saving rates is still unknown.

China's high saving rate has received much interest and has raised concerns in both policy and research communities. The high saving rate of households, enterprises, and the government has facilitated the high investment rates that have fueled China's rapid growth, but it has also aroused worries about the imbalance between investment and domestic consumption. Cross-country empirical comparisons suggest that China's high saving rate is policy driven, because one would otherwise expect it to decline with industrialization and urbanization (Kuijs 2005, 2006). Moreover, the macroeconomics literature suggests that reducing savings may be favorable for China's sustained economic growth and may help realize balanced growth (Blanchard and Giavazzi 2006; Hofman and Kuijs 2007).

Macroeconomists have adapted life-cycle theories to explain high household saving rates in China. The life-cycle saving hypothesis predicts that saving rates will be higher when one is young than when one is old. Therefore, a younger population age structure will lead to higher saving rates. China's demographic transition is unique in its pace (see chapter 1). China's baby boom of the late 1950s and 1960s and the implementation of family planning policies in the 1970s have resulted in a population age structure favorable for high saving rates since the 1980s and have provided a "demographic dividend" (Cai and Wang 2005). Market-oriented reforms and development strategy adjustments have created an institutional environment favorable for harvesting the demographic dividend. The rising saving rate is associated with a declining dependency ratio from the mid-1980s onward and can be expected to fall with the acceleration of population aging (Modigliani and Cao 2004).

Microeconomic studies have paid more attention to increasing risk and uncertainty facing households during economic transition, and they suggest that risk and uncertainty may have contributed to the rising saving rates of rural and urban households. Breaking the "iron rice bowl" through the reforms of the 1990s brought about unemployment risk and raised the uncertainty faced by urban households. To cope with potential layoff and dislocation, urban households increased their precautionary savings (Meng 2003). From 1995 to 2005, the average urban household saving rate in China rose by 7 percentage points, to about one-quarter of disposable income. The unusual age pattern of saving rates, in which younger and older households save more than middle-aged households, reflects the rising private burden of expenditures on housing, education, and health care, which may be felt more keenly as a result of credit constraints and financial underdevelopment (Chamon and Prasad 2010). In rural areas, only about 10 percent of savings of rural households can be attributed to precaution against natural risks, and migration has reduced exposure to this source of risk by providing an alternative source of income (Giles and Yoo 2007). Thus, precautionary saving against weather-related shocks in rural areas may have fallen even as saving rates continued to rise.[1]

The sharp decline in the rural saving rate in recent years may be driven by a reduction in two other motives for saving: (a) the cost of compulsory education and (b) the potential cost of health shocks. In recent years, the government introduced policies to provide free compulsory education to rural residents and to lower exposure to financial risk associated with health shocks by establishing the New Cooperative Medical System. These policy measures may reduce burdens on rural households and reduce the precautionary motive for saving associated with the potential for high health care costs. Changes in the composition of rural consumption show that education expenditures dropped from 12.1 percent in 2003 to 8.6 percent in 2008, but that health and medical expenditures increased from 6.0 percent to 6.7 percent over the same period. The proportion of food expenditures dropped from 45.6 percent in 2003 to 43.7 percent in 2008, but the proportion of other expenditures, including clothing, housing, durable goods, communications, and transportation, increased over that period.

In rural areas, high saving rates are positively correlated with high income. Figure 4.2 shows average saving rates of rural households by income quintile for 2003 and 2007. In 2007, rural households in the highest income group saved 40 percent of their capita income, whereas those in the lowest income group dissaved at a rate of −37.4 percent, presumably to smooth their consumption. The difference in saving rates across the second, third, and fourth income groups is about 10 percent for each. Saving rates for each income quintile decreased by 2007 compared with those of 2003, but the magnitude of the decrease was greatest for the lowest quintile. These patterns for saving are consistent with predictions of the permanent income hypothesis in an environment in which household incomes vary considerably (Deaton 1990; Paxson 1992). In years with large positive shocks to income, saving rates would be high; in years with sharp negative shocks, one would expect significant dissaving.

Figure 4.2   Rural Saving Rates, by Income Quintile

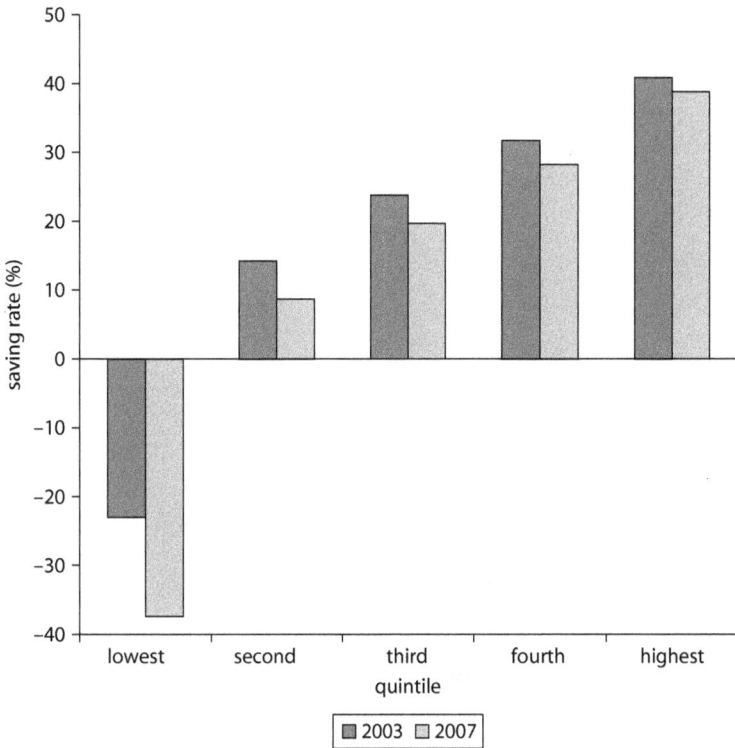

Sources: NBS 2005b, 2008.
Note: Savings = disposable income (or net income) − consumption expenditure.

Saving Behavior and Migration

This section uses a recent subsample of the Research Center for Rural Economy (RCRE) panel to examine how saving patterns vary with the presence of migrant family members.[2] First, two definitions of household savings suggested by Paxson (1992) are compared. In the first, savings equals net income minus consumption expenditure, whereas the second treats expenditures on durable goods and housing as a form of savings. These two definitions produce different rural saving rates, although they have very similar trends. Figure 4.3 shows that the saving rate of rural households was 34.4 percent in 2003 and rose to 40.6 percent in 2005. It then dropped to 37.3 percent in 2006. If one compares saving rates from RCRE households with National Bureau of Statistics data, the

Figure 4.3   Rural Household Saving Rates, 2003–06

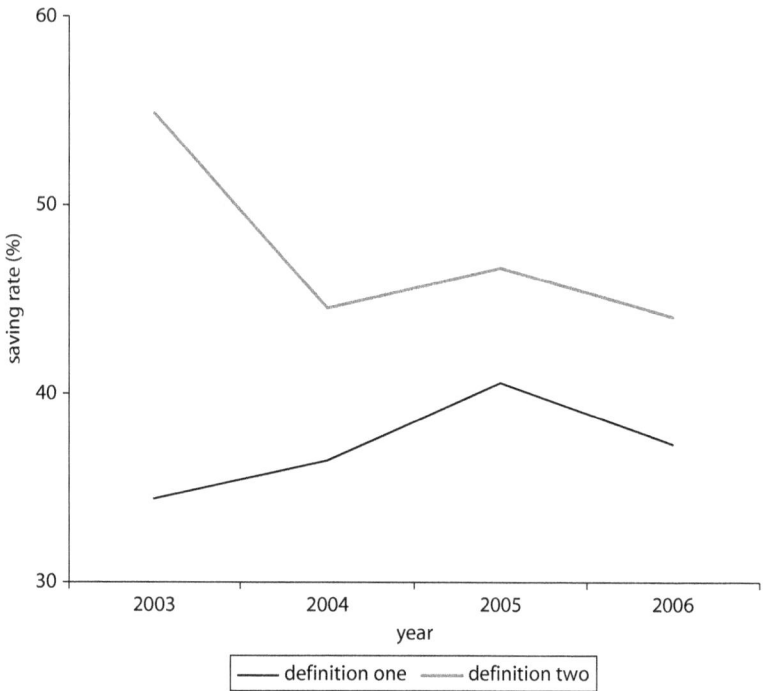

Source: Research Center for Rural Economy (RCRE), Ministry of Agriculture (MOA), Repeated Household Data (various years).
Note: Definition one = net income – consumption expenditure; definition two = definition one + housing expenditure + durable goods expenditure.

former are higher by 8.5 to 19.1 percentage points. The following analysis uses the first definition of savings to examine the saving profile of rural households over the age distribution, by migration status of family members and by social security coverage.

Households without elderly members have had higher saving rates than those with them, although the gap appears to have narrowed in recent years. Figure 4.4 compares the saving rates of rural households with and without elderly members. From 2003 to 2006, rural households without elderly saved more than those with elderly. In 2003, the saving rate of rural households without elderly was 36.3 percent, whereas it was 29.8 percent for those with elderly, a difference of 6.5 percentage points. In 2006, the saving rates of rural households with and without elderly were 35.7 percent and 38.2 percent, respectively, dropping by 2.4 percentage

Figure 4.4   Saving Rates of Rural Households with and without Elderly, 2003–06

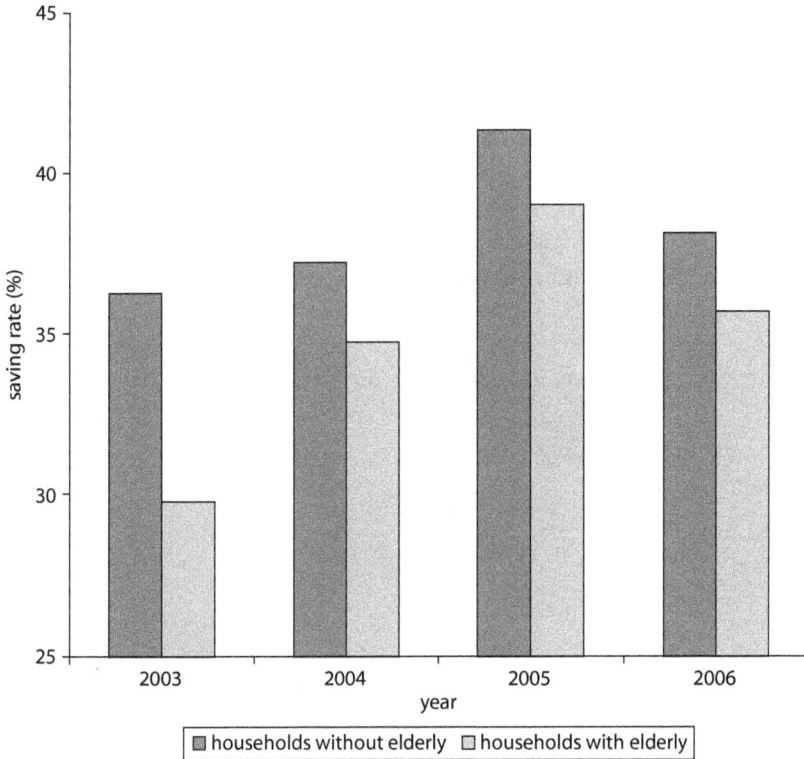

Source: RCRE, MOA, Repeated Household Data (various years).
Note: Savings = net income − consumption expenditure.

points. These descriptive statistics are consistent with a prediction from life-cycle theory that families with a higher number of elderly members are likely to save less than those with younger adults.

Higher average saving rates among households with migrants might be expected for three reasons. First, households with migrants have more insurance against negative income shocks and thus will tend to dissave less than households without migrants when hit by such shocks. Second, rural households are to some extent "permanent income savers." If income remitted from a migrant family member is viewed as transitory (or at least less permanent), then one may expect households with migrants to save remittances. Third, migration may be driven in part by credit market failures, and migrant family members may save migrant earnings in anticipation of investing in housing or durable goods. In this case, migration and saving decisions are made jointly, and one would expect to see higher saving among families with migrants.[3]

From 2003 to 2006, rural households with migrants had higher saving rates than those without migrants. Figure 4.5 shows the saving rates for rural households with and without migrants. In 2003, the saving rates of rural households with and without migrants were 37.4 percent and 30.8 percent, respectively, a difference of 6.6 percentage points. The largest difference between rural households with and without migrants was 13.0 percentage points in 2005.

Saving rates of rural households with elderly are also higher if they have migrants. As shown in figure 4.6, the saving rates of households with elderly members that have migrants are higher than those without migrants, and the difference between the two rates fluctuates over time.

Figure 4.5   Saving Rates of Rural Households with and without Migration, 2003–06

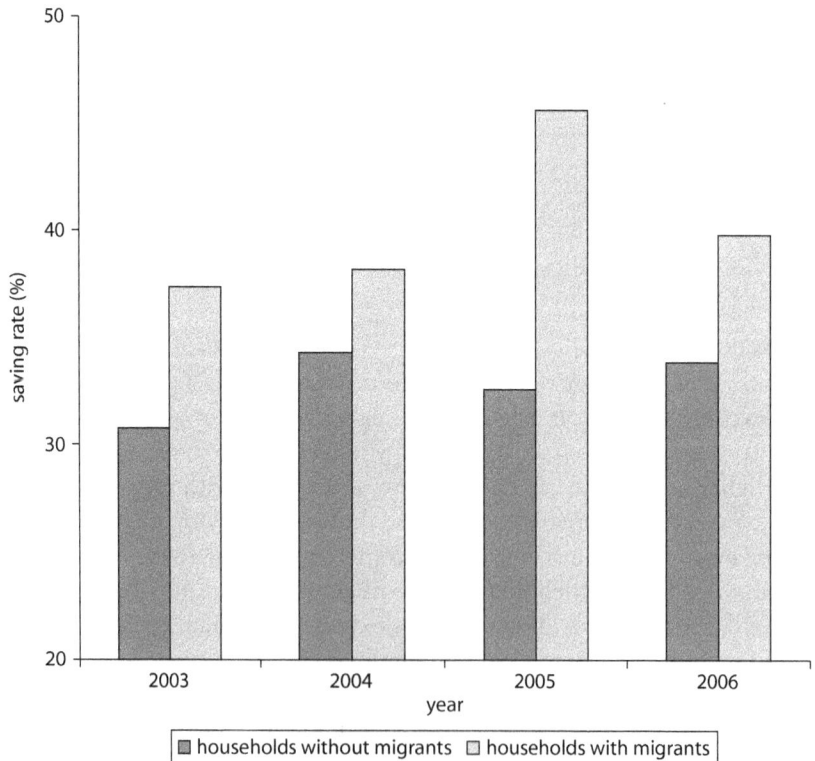

Source: RCRE, MOA, Repeated Household Data, estimated by Cai, Giles, and Wang 2009.

Figure 4.6   Saving Rates of Rural Households with Elderly, with and without Migration, 2003–06

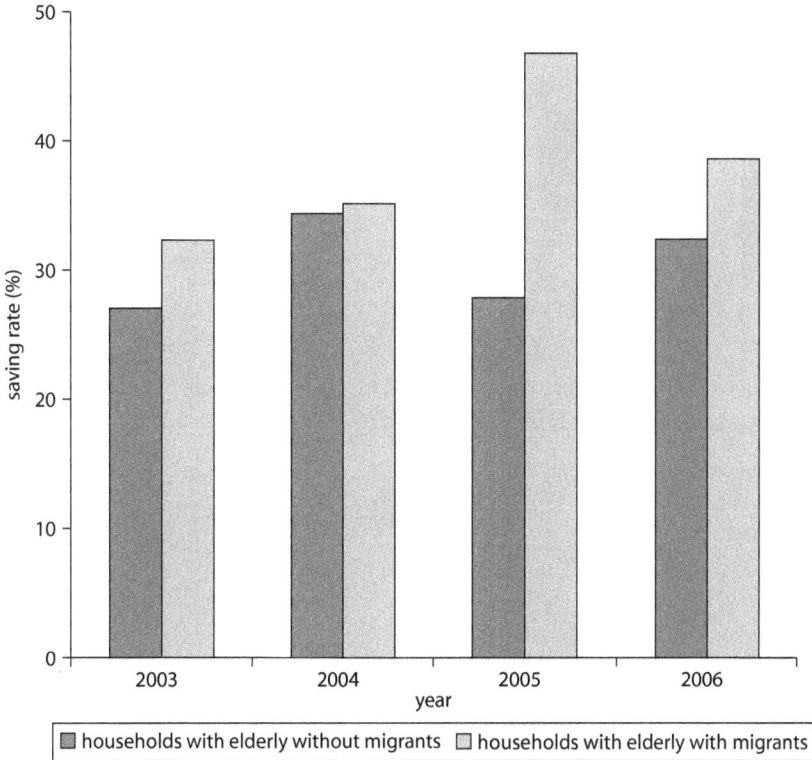

Source: RCRE, MOA, Repeated Household Data, estimated by Cai, Giles, and Wang 2009.

In 2003, the saving rate of rural households with elderly and with migrants was 32.3 percent, 5.3 percentage points higher than those without migrants. The gap between saving rates in 2004 was much smaller at 0.8 percentage points; but by 2005, it was 19.0 percent before falling again to 6.2 percent in 2006.

As might be predicted, saving rates change over the life cycle. Figure 4.7 shows life-cycle patterns in the saving decisions of rural households and the resulting nonlinear relationship between saving rates and age.[4] Although saving rates were higher for all ages in 2006, life-cycle patterns over the age distribution were similar. In 2006, the saving rate decreased from age 20 to 40, but increased from 40 to 55, and then steadily declined with age after 55. High saving rates among the young in urban China are frequently explained by the high cost of

Figure 4.7   Saving Rates of Rural Households, 2003 and 2006

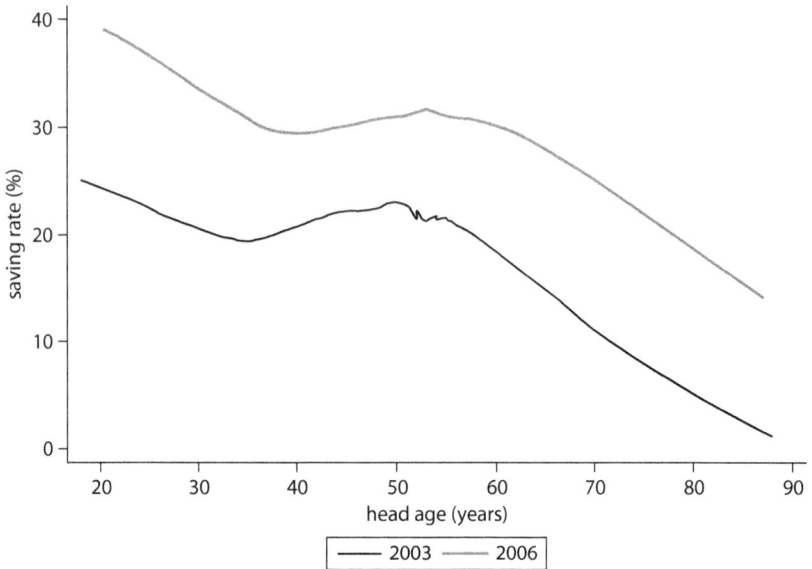

Source: RCRE, MOA, Repeated Household Data, estimated by Cai, Giles, and Wang 2009.

housing and imperfect credit markets, and housing and durable goods costs likely contribute to high savings among the rural young as well (Chamon and Prasad 2010). Marriage-market competition in a world of rising male-female sex ratios may exert further upward pressure on housing prices in this environment and create further incentives for saving (Wei and Zhang 2011). The decline in saving rates among the old is consistent with standard life-cycle theory, although on average, saving remains positive well into old age.

As shown in figure 4.8, the saving rate of rural households with migrants declines little with age, but an earlier and more pronounced decrease occurs for elderly households without migrants. Across the age distribution, saving rates and evidence of life-cycle saving differ considerably across households with and without migrants. The higher saving rates of elderly with migrant family members likely reflects less dissaving in the face of extreme shocks to health or earning and is likely related to the perceived transitory nature of remittance income.

The difference in saving behavior between rural households with and without social insurance is significant and consistent over time—households with social insurance have notably lower saving rates. Figure 4.9 shows the saving rates of rural households with and without

Figure 4.8   Saving Rates of Rural Households with and without Migrants, 2006

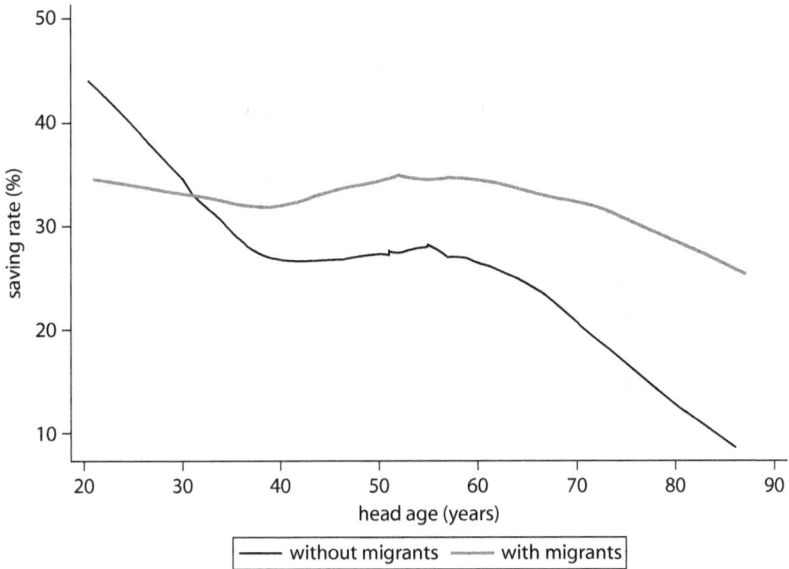

Source: RCRE, MOA, Repeated Household Data, estimated by Cai, Giles, and Wang 2009.

Figure 4.9   Saving Rates of Rural Households with and without Social Insurance

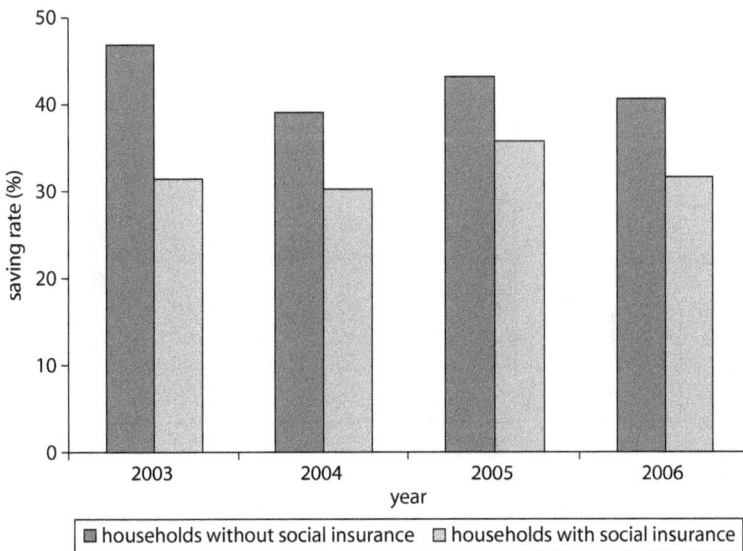

Source: RCRE, MOA, Repeated Household Data, estimated by Cai, Giles, and Wang 2009.

social insurance from 2003 to 2006.[5] As discussed earlier, the provision of social insurance can make individuals and households feel more secure about spending, which helps reduce household savings. Therefore, it is not surprising that rural households receiving social insurance benefits have a lower saving rate compared with those without benefits.

The evidence from the quintile income groups further confirms that rural households with social insurance save less than those without coverage. In figure 4.10, the highest income group has the greatest saving rate: rural households without social insurance save 51.3 percent of household income, whereas those with benefits save 42.6 percent of household income. However, the largest difference in saving rates lies in the lowest income group, which has a 23.8 percentage point difference in saving rates between rural households with and without social insurance participation.

Conclusion

Saving rate patterns of rural households differ significantly over the age distribution, by migration status of family members and by social security coverage. Rural households without elderly members have higher saving

Figure 4.10   Saving Rates of Rural Households with and without Social Insurance, 2006, by Quintile

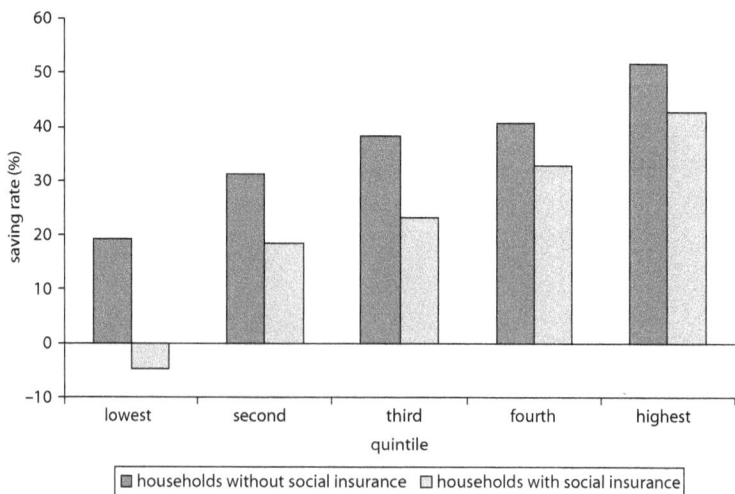

Source: RCRE, MOA, Repeated Household Data, estimated by Cai, Giles, and Wang 2009.

rates, although the gap is narrowing, and those with migrant members have higher saving rates than those without. As might be expected, the saving rate declines with age after 55, but the average saving rate is always positive, even into advanced old age. Little comparable decline occurs in saving rates in elderly households with migrants, which likely reflects the perceived transitory nature of remittance income. The difference in saving behavior between rural households with and without social insurance benefits is significant and consistent over time, which is further verified when findings are broken down by income quintile.

Saving provides an informal mechanism for individuals and rural households to cope with uncertainty and risk. As discussed in this chapter, the high saving rate in China is probably related to increasing risk and uncertainty facing households during economic transition. Given that the Chinese government strongly emphasizes the welfare of ordinary people as it tries to rebalance the economy, recent initiatives to expand the rural safety net and social insurance system are welcome instruments not only for supporting household welfare, particularly for elderly households, but also as economic tools to help reduce precautionary motives for saving and to boost consumption.

Notes

1. Wei and Zhang (2011) provide compelling evidence that China's high saving rate may be driven, in part, by rising male-female sex ratios. As the sex ratio rises, Chinese parents with a son raise their savings in a competitive manner to improve their son's relative attractiveness for marriage. The pressure on savings spills over to other households.

2. The analysis draws on a different subsample of eight provinces, including Anhui, Chongqing, Guangdong, Jiangsu, Jilin, Shandong, Shanxi, and Xinjiang, with 4,100–4,600 rural households surveyed annually between 2003 and 2006.

3. Alternatively, a data issue may be driving the observation: the RCRE household survey asks about the earnings and expenditures of migrants as part of the household survey. If expenditures of migrants are not observed as well as incomes, this exclusion will lead to mechanically higher saving rates among migrant households, although net income for migrants is used in this analysis.

4. This measurement uses a nonparametric locally weighted regression of saving rates against the age of the household head.

5. Household expenditures for insurance (including asset insurance, life insurance, production insurance, education insurance, and pension insurance) are used to identify whether rural households have social insurance.

References

Blanchard, Olivier, and Francesco Giavazzi. 2006. "Rebalancing Growth in China: A Three-Handed Approach." *China & World Economy* 14 (4): 1–20.

Cai, Fang, John Giles, and Dewen Wang. 2009. "The Well-Being of China's Rural Elderly." Background Paper for East Asia Social Protection Team, World Bank, Washington, DC.

Cai, Fang, and Dewen Wang. 2005. "China's Demographic Transition: Implications for Growth." In *The China Boom and Its Discontents*, ed. Ross Garnaut and Ligang Song, 34–52. Canberra, Australia: Asia Pacific Press.

Chamon, Marcos, and Eswar Prasad. 2010. "Why Are Saving Rates of Urban Households in China Rising?" American Economic Journal: macroeconomics 2 (1): 93–130.

Deaton, Angus. 1990. "Saving in Developing Countries: Theory and Review." In *Proceedings of the World Bank Annual Conference on Development Economics, 1989*, supplement to the *The World Bank Economic Review* and *The World Bank Research Observer*, Washington, DC: World Bank: 61–96.

Giles, John, and Kyeongwon Yoo. 2007. "Precautionary Behavior, Migrant Networks and Household Consumption Decisions: An Empirical Analysis Using Household Panel Data from Rural China." *Review of Economics and Statistics* 89 (3): 534–51.

Hofman, Bert, and Louis Kuijs. 2007. "Rebalancing China's Growth." Paper presented at the conference on China's Exchange Rate Policy, Peterson Institute for International Economics, Washington, DC, October 19.

Kuijs, Louis. 2005. "Investment and Saving in China." Policy Research Working Paper 3633, World Bank, Washington, DC.

———. 2006. "How Will China's Saving-Investment Balance Evolve?" Policy Research Working Paper 3958, World Bank, Washington, DC.

Meng, Xin. 2003. "Unemployment, Consumption Smoothing, and Precautionary Saving in Urban China." *Journal of Comparative Economics* 31 (3): 465–85.

Modigliani, Franco, and Shi Larry Cao. 2004. "The Chinese Saving Puzzle and the Life-Cycle Hypothesis." *Journal of Economic Literature* 42 (1): 145–70.

NBS (National Bureau of Statistics). 2005a. *China Population Statistics Yearbook 2005*. Beijing: China Statistics Press.

———. 2005b. *China's Rural Household Survey Yearbook 2005*. Beijing: China Statistics Press.

———. 2008. *China's Rural Household Survey Yearbook 2008*. Beijing: China Statistics Press.

———. 2009. *China Population and Employment Statistics Yearbook*. Beijing: China Statistics Press.

Paxson, Christina H. 1992. "Using Weather Variability to Estimate the Response of Savings to Transitory Income in Thailand." *American Economic Review* 82 (1): 15–33.

RCRE (Research Center for Rural Economy). Various years. *Rural Household Surveys* for 2003–2006 from Anhui, Chongqing, Guangdong, Jiangsu, Jilin, Shandong, Shanxi, and Xinjiang. Beijing: Ministry of Agriculture, RCRE.

Wei, Shangjin, and Xiaobo Zhang. 2011. "The Competitive Saving Motive: Evidence from Rising Sex Ratios and Savings Rates in China." *Journal of Political Economy* 119 (3): 511–64.

CHAPTER 5

Evolution of the Rural Pension System in China

The previous chapters of this book examined various aspects of the welfare of the rural elderly in China. On the basis of findings on poverty and vulnerability, sources of support for the rural elderly, demographic trends, and saving behavior, the rural poor clearly are unusually subject to poverty and are also highly dependent on private sources (primarily their own labor and family support) to sustain adequate levels of welfare in old age. The analysis also showed that a number of trends suggest that the challenges of sustaining rural welfare may increase in coming years, even in the face of continued solid growth. The evidence thus supports a rationale for public intervention through transfers for the rural elderly, which should not crowd out private sources of support too significantly. A further important dimension in the discussion of public intervention in support of the rural elderly is the broader desire of Chinese policy makers to rebalance their economy toward greater emphasis on domestic demand, a shift that may be inhibited by high levels of precautionary

This chapter was prepared by Philip O'Keefe, based on a background study for this report by Wu (2009), which includes a literature review, a policy assessment, and detailed reviews of current rural pension pilots in selected cities (Beijing, Baoji in Shaanxi Province, Yantai in Shandong Province, and Suzhou in Anhui Province).

saving among both the rural working-age rural population and the elderly. In that light, a macroeconomic rationale may also underlie recent government efforts to expand public transfers for the rural elderly, thus helping reduce overly high levels of saving and freeing private resources for consumption during working life and in old age.

A key policy tool for improving welfare of the rural elderly, with which the Chinese authorities have experimented on and off over the past two decades, is a widespread rural pension system. In recent years, this system has received renewed impetus with the commitment of the 16th plenary meeting of the Communist Party of China (CPC) in 2006 to establish a comprehensive social security system that will cover all urban and rural residents by 2020. This commitment is reflected in the Law on Social Insurance of 2010, which provides the legal framework for a pension scheme for rural residents. State Council Document 1 of 2009 endorsed accelerated efforts for "establishing a new rural pension system, which is to be financed from individual contributions, collective subsidy and government subsidy" (State Council 2009a). These commitments are reflected in the introduction of a national rural pension pilot in the second half of 2009 that covered 23 percent of counties by the end of 2010 and is expected to achieve full geographic coverage by the end of 2012. A scheme for urban residents with a similar design became national policy in June 2011, adding to the significance of considering the rural pension scheme design. This chapter outlines the evolution of the Chinese rural pension system over the past two decades, with a particular focus on provincial pilots during the 2000s and the national pilot.

The evolution of the rural pension system in China can be divided into four main phases: (a) an initiation and expansion phase from 1986 to 1998, (b) a contraction and stagnation phase from 1999 to 2002, (c) a renewal phase of piloting toward development of a national rural pension system (2003 to 2009), and (d) the national rural pension pilot from 2009 onward. Each phase is discussed in turn below.

Initiation and Expansion of Rural Pensions: 1986–98

The initial exploration of rural pensions was set out in the Seventh Five-Year Plan (1986–90), which noted that "efforts should be made to study how to establish a rural pension system, launch and gradually expand pilot schemes in line with economic development" (State Council 1986, 193–94). This endeavor was built on through county-level pilots led by the Ministry of Civil Affairs (MOCA) in Beijing and in Shanxi Province, which emphasized mixed financing responsibility among government, collectives, and individuals, with most of the responsibility falling on individuals. The pilots were followed in 1991 by (a) the State Council's issuing Document 33, "Decision on Establishing a Unified Basic Old Age Insurance for Enterprise Employees," which designated MOCA to take the lead on rural pensions and (b) MOCA's launching pilots in five counties of Shandong Province.

A clear policy push occurred in the early 1990s to expand rural pension schemes. The various pilots contributed to a major policy document in 1992 from MOCA: "Basic Scheme for Rural Pension at County Level" (referred to hereafter as the Basic Scheme). The Basic Scheme was elaborated on in a subsequent policy document in 1995,[1] which outlined a set of basic principles for rural pension schemes while allowing for variations in specifics by localities:

- Schemes were to be voluntary, mainly financed from individual contributions, supported by contributions from collectives at the village and township levels, and supported by preferential government policies (for example, tax relief for collectives on contributions). The Basic Scheme set the retirement age at 60 for both men and women, although in the practices that emerged, the retirement age for women was not uncommonly set at 55.
- Following the lead of the urban pension system reform, schemes were to be based on funded individual accounts.
- Individual contributions were to range from 2 to 20 yuan monthly with a matching 2 yuan contributed by the collective.
- Elderly farmers were entitled to receive a pension until death. In cases in which they lived fewer than 10 years after retiring, any balances in their individual accounts could be inherited.[2]
- Investments of accumulated contributions were to be made in bank deposits and national bonds; no direct investments were otherwise allowed. Although portfolio rules mandated low-return investments, in practice the system committed to a guaranteed rate of return.
- The local Bureau of Civil Affairs would administer the scheme, and administrative costs would be covered from contributions (with a cap of 3 percent set subsequently).
- Oversight and regulation of the scheme were to sit largely with the implementing agency (that is, MOCA at the county level), subject to the internal controls of the Ministry of Finance and internal auditing.

As a result of this policy initiative, coverage of rural pensions expanded significantly during the 1990s, with programs established by the end of 1998 in 31 provinces and 2,123 counties (just under three-quarters of all rural counties). This period was also the high point of coverage, with 80.25 million rural worker participants and more than 600,000 pension beneficiaries. However, concerns soon began to emerge about the operation of local schemes and the lack of a sound governance framework; the Asian financial crisis in 1997 underscored the need to rethink the program.[3] Responsibility for rural pensions was subsequently switched from MOCA to the Ministry of Labor and Social Security (MOLSS; now the Ministry of Human Resources and Social Security) in the 1998 administrative restructuring.

Contraction and Stagnation: 1999–2002

Because of concerns about the effectiveness and sustainability of rural pension schemes, a sharp policy shift occurred in the late 1990s to limit their expansion. The change in the official position on rural pensions was reflected in the 1999 State Council declaration that China was not yet ready for universal rural pensions, which directed counties to (a) cease expanding schemes; (b) rectify the operations of existing schemes; and (c) when possible, transfer schemes to the management of commercial insurers. By 2001, the shift in policy contributed to a sharp decline in coverage to just under 60 million participants, with the number stabilizing between 50 million and 55 million through 2007 in roughly 1,900 counties. Despite this contraction, new participants continued to enter the system and accumulated funds from existing schemes continued to increase, more than doubling from 2000 to over 41 billion yuan in 2007. The number of pension beneficiaries approached 4 million by 2007 as existing schemes matured (see table 5.1). The variability of indicators over time is noteworthy, especially during the 1990s.

The development of the rural pension system during this phase was characterized by several deficiencies that undermined the achievement of policy objectives:

- Coverage was highly imbalanced geographically, with four coastal provinces (Jiangsu, Shandong, Shanghai, and Zhejiang) accounting for about 45 percent of total participation and 64 percent of total accumulations. Poorer regions, in contrast, generally failed to attain significant penetration.

Table 5.1   Rural Pension Indicators, 1993–2007

| Year | Number of participants (millions) | | | Counties | Number of recipients (millions) | Accumulated funds (yuan, billions) |
	Year-end total	New participants	New participants employed in township enterprises			
1993	n.a.	n.a.	n.a.	1,100	n.a.	1.48
1994	34.84	n.a.	n.a.	n.a.	0.17	2.70
1995	51.43	n.a.	n.a.	n.a.	0.27	5.95
1996	65.94	n.a.	n.a.	n.a.	0.32	9.95
1997	74.52	n.a.	n.a.	2,100	0.61	13.92
1998	80.25	n.a.	n.a.	2,123	n.a.	16.62
1999	80.00	n.a.	n.a.	n.a.	n.a.	n.a.
2000	61.72	1.84	1.51	2,052	0.98	19.55
2001	59.95	3.12	0.92	2,045	1.08	21.61
2002	54.62	4.13	0.67	1,955	1.23	23.32
2003	54.28	2.24	1.40	1,870	1.98	25.93
2004	53.78	3.97	0.37	1,887	2.05	28.50
2005	54.42	2.34	0.29	1,990	3.02	31.00
2006	53.73	n.a.	n.a.	1,905	3.55	35.40
2007	51.71	3.06	0.19	n.a.	3.91	41.20

Sources: NBS 2009, 2008, 2007, 2006, 2006, 2004, 2003, 2002; Bulletins of Ministry of Civil Affairs (1993–97) and Ministry of Labor and Social Security (1998–2007).

- Although the policy indicated that participation was voluntary, local authorities in many cases mandated participation in the face of disinterest from farmers.
- Matching contributions from collectives were seldom made, and their incidence was highly skewed toward a small number of richer provinces. The privatization of township and village enterprises in the 1990s contributed to the lack of matching contributions from employers. As a result, 98.5 percent of matching contributions were concentrated in only five provinces (the four coastal provinces noted above plus Beijing).
- At the local level, concerns arose about the concentration of matching funds for cadre members rather than for all scheme members.[4]
- Compared with the urban scheme, in which administrative costs are borne by the government, the 3 percent administrative fee on rural schemes was deducted from farmer contributions, which was considered inequitable.
- Many schemes were unable to pay benefits in full, with at least 200 counties cancelling schemes and contributors being unable to recoup

their contributions. Even when benefits continued to be paid, they were frequently significantly less than expected because of low returns on accumulations. Low returns stemmed partly from a preponderance of investments in bank deposits with very low interest rates. The reluctance to invest in higher-return government securities was exacerbated by localized problems with fund management. As examples, Beijing and Hebei lost significant amounts of invested accumulations through the bankruptcy of fund management companies entrusted to invest in government securities.

- Supervision of schemes was weak. MOLSS figures for the end of 2000 indicate that about 20 percent of accumulations had been invested in unauthorized assets, including real estate, stocks, enterprise bonds, and nonbank financial agencies. Although local implementers may have intended to increase returns and meet guaranteed return directives, their failure to abide by investment guidelines indicates significant regulatory issues. This failure was in part a structural problem because local implementers were under the direct authority of local governments, but the scheme, in principle, was under the bureau at a higher level.
- The ratio of guaranteed rates of return, interest rates on investments, and inflation showed significant volatility, which contributed to significant negative real returns on accumulations in some periods and the reverse in others (see table 5.2).
- Pension benefits were very low, with the average pension at about 85 yuan per month in 2007. Moreover, benefits were highly variable across provinces and individuals. A general lack of confidence in schemes also

Table 5.2   Rates of Return on Accumulations and Bank Deposits, Compared with Inflation Rate

percent

Indicator	Year.Month							
	1991.1	1993.5	1994.1	1997.1	1998.1	1998.7	1999.7	2007.1
Interest rate for accumulation	8.80	8.80	12.00	8.80	6.80	5.00	2.50	3.15
Interest rate—one year's deposit in bank	8.64	9.18 (10.98 July)	10.98	7.47	5.67	4.77	2.25	2.52 (4.14 year end)
Inflation rate	3.40	14.70	24.10	2.80	−0.80	−0.80	−1.40	4.80

Source: Wu 2009.

resulted in very small contributions in excess of the minimum by farmers. For example, if farmers chose to contribute 2 yuan per month, their estimated pension after 15 years, in nominal terms, would have amounted to about 10 yuan per month (G. Wang 2000). Taking into account inflation and administrative costs, their real benefits would have been even less.

- The planned transfer of administration to labor bureaus was not undertaken in a timely manner (or at all in some areas), with 350 counties not having transferred management by 2007.

Renewal: 2003–09

Renewed impetus toward a new rural pension system emerged in late 2002 with the CPC Congress, which resulted in new guidelines from MOLSS (2003). This push was followed by (a) opinions of the Central Party Committee and the State Council at the end of 2005, which were part of the wider commitment to "building a new socialist countryside," and (b) the 2006 plenary meeting of the 16th CPC, which committed the government to universal social insurance coverage by 2020. Between 2003 and 2009, additional rural pension schemes developed, with more than 300 counties in 25 provinces establishing new schemes by the end of 2008.

The new rural pension schemes established during this period fall broadly into three types: (a) social pooling plus individual accounts, (b) flat universal pensions combined with individual accounts, and (c) individual accounts only. In addition, the schemes differed in the financing role of government at the accumulation and payout stages. As a result, five variants existed by 2009 when the new national pilot was announced (and into which such schemes should eventually be merged):[5]

- *Flat pensions plus individual accounts with government financing at the payout stage only.* Under this variant, individual contributions went to individual accounts, whereas the government financed flat pensions from general revenues. The most notable example of this model has been Beijing since 2005 (Beijing Municipal Government 2005). This variant was taken a step further in 2009 with further revision of the scheme to expand coverage of the rural pension to urban residents not covered by work-related urban schemes (Beijing Municipal Government 2007, 2009).

• *Flat pensions plus individual accounts with government financing (a) by matching contributions to individual accounts and (b) at the payout stage through the financing of flat pensions from general revenues.* This model has been observed, for example, in Baoji in Shaanxi Province since 2007 (a city in which 74 percent of the population is farmers) and in Qian'an in Hebei Province. In large measure, this model is the precursor to the new national pilot structure.

• *Individual accounts with social pooling with government financing at the accumulation phase.* This model is similar to the urban employee pension system but with lower contributions and fewer benefits. This model has typically been implemented in regions with high urbanization rates and good fiscal positions, such as Suzhou in Jiangsu Province since 2003 (in which 60 percent of the population is rural and a large proportion is migrant) (Suzhou Municipal Government 2003) and in Qingdao in Shandong Province.

• *Individual accounts combined with social pooling with government financing (a) by matching contributions to individual accounts and (b) at the payout stage.* This model has been implemented in Zhongshan and Dongguan.

• *Individual accounts only with government matching for contributions to individual accounts.* This model is the simplest design, although it lacks risk pooling of any form. It has been implemented in Yantai in Shandong Province since 2005 (a city in which 58 percent of the population is farmers) (Yantai Municipal Government 2007) and in Hangshou in Zhejiang Province.

In addition to these most common models, other experiments with rural pensions have been conducted, including the "land for pensions" schemes. Wen Jiang County of Chengdu Prefecture, for example, allowed farmers to enter the urban pension system under the so-called two give-ups approach, whereby farmers relinquish the management rights on their land and the use of the land on which they dwell. Similar approaches were taken in Chongqing and within Guangdong Province. Finally, schemes are being implemented for specific subgroups of farmers, particularly farmers whose land has been expropriated, and migrant workers in urban areas. This approach is common in areas experiencing rapid urbanization (even in less developed provinces, such as Ningxia) and offers entitlements in the urban system as effective compensation for expropriated land.

The preceding discussion suggests a rich history of experimentation with rural pensions in China in the lead-up to the 2009 national pilot. Such experimentation is not surprising given the wider commitment of the Chinese authorities to balanced development and development of a rural social protection system. From this experience, a number of patterns and issues emerge, which are discussed below. They are useful in considering the ways in which the recent national pilot deals with various issues and has built on previous experience.

- *Voluntary with incentives.* In policy terms, all schemes have been voluntary, relying on a mixture of incentives to encourage participation. At the same time, a feature in a number of schemes (for example, in Suzhou and Baoji) has been the system of so-called family binding, whereby the pension eligibility of an older contributor close to retirement age is determined by whether his or her spouse and all adult children contribute to the new system. Opinions differ among local commentators on the merits of this feature, although it has been adopted in the national pilot.[6] Apart from this feature, the new rural pension schemes have been incentive driven through the subsidy mechanism, although some debate exists on the extent to which any program with sufficiently strong support from the local administration is truly "voluntary." The incentive-based approach has resulted in extensive coverage in a number of pilots. For example, Beijing's participation rate rose from 37 percent to 85 percent following an increase in the subsidy level, whereas in Suzhou—where government contributions constitute 60 percent of the combined total—participation has reached 99 percent. Examples like Baoji are more nuanced, with a 68 percent participation rate among all farmers, rising to 92 percent for farmers over 45 years of age.

- *Retirement ages and contribution requirements.* As noted, the prescribed retirement age under the former Basic Scheme was 60 for both sexes, and participation started at 20 years of age. The retirement age has varied at both ends under the new pilot schemes—with the entry age for participation as low as 16 in Beijing and 18 in Baoji (although it remains 20 in places such as Yantai) and the retirement age set at 55 for women and 60 for men in Beijing, at 59 for both sexes in Yantai, and with no upper age limit in Baoji. A clear issue here for localities seeking

to integrate urban and rural systems is the retirement ages in urban
systems, which are typically 55 for women and 60 for men.

Requiring a 15-year contribution history to qualify for full benefits
under pilot schemes has been a widespread practice, with the obvious
exception of individual account–only schemes, in which minimum
contribution periods are irrelevant. However, a number of schemes
recognize the transition issue and have incorporated special treatment
for those older than 45. For example, Baoji has allowed a full pension
for those over 45 if they contribute until age 60; those over 60 are also
entitled, subject to "family binding" (a feature adopted in the new
national pilot). Some schemes also made provisions for the lump-sum
payment of contributions by those without a full contribution history—in some cases at the point of retirement (for example, Beijing and
Zhuhai) and in others during the accumulation phase. Other schemes
have allowed older cohorts to continue to make contributions for up
to five years after reaching the normal retirement age.

- *Financing models and sustainability.* A key feature of all the pilot schemes
  in this period was significant public subsidies, either for contributions
  to individual accounts or during the payout phase, or both. This feature
  represents a major shift and recognition by central and local authorities
  that some form of matching is necessary to incentivize participation by
  rural populations.[7] This experience has also been addressed in part in
  the Chinese literature, and the need for public subsidies to support
  rural pension schemes is generally recognized.[8]

  Although the large majority of public subsidies have come from
  general revenues, some experiments with partial funding from dedi-
  cated revenue streams have also been conducted. Zhuhai City pio-
  neered this approach beginning in 2006 by allocating land transaction
  revenues to finance a reserve fund for incremental pensions and for
  those who exhaust their individual account accumulations.[9]

  A major and still unresolved issue is the fiscal sustainability of different scheme designs. Simulations using government spending ranging from 1.0 to 2.5 percent of general revenues have been conducted
  with different system parameters. These analyses indicate that a broad-
  based rural pension system should be fiscally affordable and sustainable in the aggregate, although it remains to be seen whether the
  requisite financial commitment will be met.[10] Initial reports using the
  government's own projections indicate a cost of 1.8 percent of fiscal
  expenditures (about 66 billion renminbi) in 2008 for the central

government's portion in the national pilot scheme. However, more work is needed. For example, rural mortality tables on a sufficiently disaggregated basis are needed and can be generated from census data. More important, clarity is needed on the financing responsibilities of subnational levels of government and the variable capacity of different levels to meet them.[11]

- *Contribution rates and benefit levels*. As one would expect, the structure of these local pilots, their absolute levels of contributions, and their benefit levels have varied substantially. Most schemes for which information is available have designated a range for the contribution rate made to individual accounts, which is often linked to average wages or rural incomes. Baoji has had a range of 10 percent to 30 percent of average rural income (and plans to lower the base to 5 percent), whereas Beijing had a much wider range, from 9 percent of average rural incomes to 30 percent of average urban wages. Suzhou appears to have been an exception in this regard, with a flat contribution rate and base for all contributors (either 10 percent of the rural average income or 50 percent of the average urban income). Interestingly, at least one Chinese scholar has raised the idea of farmers' being allowed to make some contributions in grain—although no such example was found in the research for this report—whereas others have proposed allocating grain subsidies paid to farmers to rural pension schemes.[12]

  With respect to benefits, an emerging practice is to pay close attention to the *dibao* level and fiscal sustainability when setting benefits for the flat pension portion of schemes. The general rule of thumb appears to be that flat pension benefits should be at or slightly above the average *dibao* threshold in the locality. Adding funded benefits is anticipated to take total pensions notably above the *dibao* level. This threshold may vary upward according to local fiscal capacity (for example, Beijing sets its flat pension portion at 35 percent of rural average income). For the individual account portion of schemes, the calculation of the payout has varied. For Beijing and Baoji, for example, the individual account benefit has been calculated by dividing the amount in the account at retirement by 139 (the same method that is used in their urban schemes—which reflects the combined assumptions of a notional life expectancy of 60 and an assumed drawdown interest rate of 4 percent; this method has also been adopted by the new national pilot). Although a similar approach has been taken elsewhere, the actuarial factor used in the calculation has varied (for example, Zhuhai has used a factor of 180, whereas Suzhou has used 120). Such variable practice strongly suggests a need for work on rural mortality tables, ideally at a disaggregated level, to ensure that this portion of the benefit is not exhausted too early (or, more likely if urban mortality rates are being used, too late).

• *Institutional issues.* The experience of local pilots in this period with respect to both scheme administration and fund management demonstrates a degree of continuity, but regulation demands greater attention. Overall administration of new schemes has remained with the Social Security Bureau, with roles also for villages (collection of contributions and, in many cases, payment of benefits), townships (consolidation of collections, approval of benefits, and registration), and counties (for general oversight and scheme design). The computerization of scheme information systems also appears to have generally improved, even in less developed areas such as Baoji. Within this general administrative structure, a variety of local innovations in administration occur. For example, Suzhou farmers have been able to contribute directly through banks rather than through village officials, and post offices (including mobile facilities) are being used in areas with lower banking penetration. Some schemes have also allowed for the seasonality of farmer incomes, so that schemes such as that in Baoji have made collections only once a year in July or August.

With respect to fund management, the Basic Scheme resources had been managed at the county level; and this practice has remained for local pilots after 2003. Some researchers have suggested the city as the appropriate level for fund management; others have proposed the provincial or even national levels (see C. Liu 2007; Z. Liu 2003; Lü 2005; and Z. Wang 2004). Portfolio rules have clearly continued to be very conservative (and remain so in the national pilot). Some researchers have proposed establishing reserve funds to cover low rates of return (although such funds are more typically used to address fluctuations in returns or the exhaustion of benefits because of longevity in funded systems). The concept of a reserve fund is, in principle, attractive, and actual practice, in places such as Zhuhai, suggests an interest.[13] The more significant concern going forward is the regulation of the funded portion of the new national scheme. As discussed earlier, regulation was a significant weakness of the old schemes, and even in the mature urban schemes, it continues to be an area in which the capacity of the system remains stretched (World Bank forthcoming a).

- *Portability between schemes.* A range of transition policies has been observed for schemes initiated in this period. The first type of transition is from old to new schemes in the same locality. Practice has differed: areas such as Beijing have allowed portability of funded accumulations from old to new schemes, whereas others, such as the province of Hunan, stipulate that participants must close their accounts in old schemes before starting afresh in new pilot schemes.[14] The second (and ultimately more important) issue is portability between rural and urban schemes (or migrant-worker schemes located in urban areas where such schemes exist). Portability will be critical in reaching the government's stated goal of an integrated social security system by 2020. The ease with which portability can be achieved has varied according to scheme design and the compatibility of rural pilots with existing urban schemes. In Suzhou, for example, a simple two-to-one rule has been used for farmers wishing to transfer their social pooling rights from the rural to the urban scheme; such transfer is easily done because the rural contribution base has been exactly half that of the urban system. In Beijing, provisions for portability have also been made, although transfer is only done at the point of retirement. If a former farmer has accumulated enough years in the urban system at retirement, he or she will enjoy an urban pension (with an allowance for lower rural contributions), whereas his or her urban contributions will be credited to the rural pension scheme if the accumulation period in the urban system is fewer than 15 years. In all schemes, the funded portion is easily made portable, in principle.

- *Interface of pensions and social assistance.* The relationship of these local rural pension schemes to various social assistance benefits also merits consideration. The most interesting example is *wubao*, a social welfare benefit that guarantees an "average" standard of living for people in the so-called three-nos category (no income, no labor capacity, no sources of family support), in which the elderly appear to be significantly over-represented.[15] In some areas, such as Suzhou, *wubao* recipients have had their individual account benefits refunded. For rural *dibao*, individuals can receive both a pension and *wubao* (because the latter is a household-level benefit), which can result in the total household income falling below the local *dibao* line even with a pensioner in a new scheme. Finally, pensions from local schemes have had no effect on the receipt of the supportive allowance for following family planning policy, although some Chinese researchers have proposed integrating the programs through the use of the family planning subsidy as an additional subsidy toward individual pension contributions (once participants are past child-bearing age) (see Mi and Yang 2008; C. Yang 2007; and Y. Yang 2007).

Looking Ahead: The Rural Pilot Program

Attention to the issue of rural pensions has shifted into high gear with the announcement in 2009 of a national rural pension pilot that started in late 2009 and aims to achieve full geographic coverage no later than 2013 (State Council 2009b). The diverse experience with rural pension schemes at the subnational level outlined earlier has offered important lessons for policy makers at the national level, which are reflected in significant measure in the design of the national pilot. The guiding principle of the pilot is *basic insurance and wide coverage with flexibility and sustainability*. The pilot started in 10 percent of counties nationwide in late 2009, with an initial aim of full geographic coverage in rural areas by 2020. However, the schedule has already been accelerated, with a target of 23 percent of counties to be included by the end of 2010 and the expectation that all counties will be covered by the end of 2012 (State Council 20011). Initial experience with take-up has been positive, with more than 36 million contributors enrolled in the first few months of implementation by Chinese New Year 2010 and approximately 13.4 million people already receiving pensions by that time. These numbers represent an estimated national participation rate of about 50 percent, with local participation rates as high as 80 to 90 percent in some areas, particularly those such as Baoji that already had mature pilots. Participation has continued to expand rapidly, with over 150 million contributors by mid-2011. The design has several key features:

- Participation by rural workers is voluntary.
- All rural residents over 16 years of age are eligible to participate if they are not already covered in a basic urban scheme.
- Participants become eligible for a pension at 60 years of age.
- The scheme provides for individual pension accounts with matching contributions and a basic flat pension for workers who, in the mature system, will have contributed for 15 years. The initial value of the basic

pension is 55 yuan per month, which can be supplemented by local governments at their discretion from their own revenues. Individual accounts will have a rate of return equal to the one-year deposit interest rate of the People's Bank of China; benefits will be computed by dividing the accumulation at age 60 by 139 (as is done in the urban workers' scheme). The indexation procedure for the basic pension is somewhat vague—to be set in accordance with "economic development and changing prices."

- At the time the scheme is introduced, those over 60 years of age can receive the basic pension benefit, provided their children are contributing to the scheme (that is, "family binding"). Those with fewer than 15 years left before reaching 60 should contribute during their working lives and can then make lump-sum contributions to make up any shortfall in the vesting period of 15 years of contributions.
- Financing of the scheme will come from a combination of (a) central subsidies to support the basic pension (in full for central and western regions and 50 percent for eastern regions); (b) individual contributions (ranging from 100 to 500 yuan annually at the worker's choice); (c) a partial match on the individual contribution by local governments of at least 30 yuan per year (independent of the contribution level chosen by the worker), or at a higher rate as shall be determined; and (d) collective subsidies, which are encouraged but not mandated, with no level specified. During the first months of implementation, contributors have most commonly chosen the 100- or the 500-yuan contribution levels. At the same time, some provinces and counties have allowed for considerably higher contribution levels from farmers of up to 2,500 yuan in some coastal areas.
- Fund management for individual account accumulations will begin at the county level, with the aim of shifting management to the provincial level as quickly as is feasible. Local offices of the Ministry of Human Resources and Social Security (MHRSS) will supervise funds.

The overall approach of the new pension pilot reflects a number of lessons from international experience and significantly improves on many earlier rural pension schemes. Matching individual account contributions—the so-called matching defined contribution, or MDC, approach—sensibly recognizes the need for incentives for rural workers to participate in pension schemes. In addition, the introduction of a basic minimum benefit echoes the practice of a number of developed and developing countries that have introduced social pensions for the elderly, although linking eligibility for the basic benefit to individual account contributions represents an important difference in approach. Finally, the role of central financing reflects lessons from other areas of social policy in China, including health insurance and *dibao*, which have clearly demonstrated the need for central subsidies to lagging regions if the equity objectives of coverage expansion are to be realized.

Although the objectives and broad design features of the rural pilot program have much to recommend them, a number of issues in the program's design may benefit from further consideration and closer evaluation as the scheme is implemented. Addressing these issues could help improve incentives, equity, portability, and fund management. The following four issues are discussed further below:

- Contribution levels, the degree of subsidy, and participation incentives
- Benefit eligibility and levels
- Fund management for the individual account part of the scheme
- Portability of benefits and system "dovetailing"

With respect to subsidies to incentivize participation, the current match of 30 yuan against the minimum 100-yuan annual contribution is low compared with emerging practices for MDCs in developing countries (where a one-to-one match is more common). The flat match also acts as a weak incentive for making contributions over the 100-yuan minimum, although it has merit from an equity perspective. A further complicating factor is that the assurance of a basic pension after the vesting period of contributions acts as a significant incentive to participate. Overall, no international consensus exists yet on the appropriate matching rate in MDC schemes. Thus, monitoring the pilot will be important to see whether the 30-yuan match is sufficient, both in incentivizing participation at the basic 100-yuan contribution level and in incentivizing higher individual contributions. This question can only be answered empirically.

The discussion of subsidies and incentives also raises the issue of the appropriate balance between ex ante subsidies (that is, the matching of individual account contributions) and ex post subsidies (that is, the provision of a basic pension benefit). Although the current emphasis on the ex post subsidy has the advantage of simplicity, it is less attractive for a mobile rural population. Once the system matures, rural workers who enroll in an urban scheme upon migration—or who intend to move—would not benefit as greatly from the incentive effect of the ex post subsidy under the current design. This consideration may be important with an increasingly mobile and urbanizing population. Increasing the ex ante subsidy by increasing matching would lessen this possible disincentive effect.

An obvious question raised by a shift in the balance of public subsidies from ex post to ex ante is its effect on the poverty alleviation objective of the basic rural pension. If greater public subsidies were shifted ex ante, maintaining a neutral fiscal effect would require a lower basic pension in a situation in which the 55-yuan benefit is already below the rural poverty line and could reduce the basic benefit below the average *dibao* level, which has additional negative incentive effects. Such a shift could be addressed in at least two ways. First, a partial benefit reduction of the basic benefit for individuals over a certain income threshold may be possible to protect the benefit level for poorer elderly people.[16] Second, the local administrative level may be able to supplement the basic benefit to ensure that it exceeds the local *dibao* level.

A second issue that merits consideration relates to fund management. The initial approach of allowing fund management at the county level has a range of drawbacks, including investment risk and the risk of accounts being in practice "empty." Such localized management complicates providing portability of account balances for rural workers who move beyond their home counties. In addition, the demographic trends in rural areas suggest that a sizable reserve fund will likely be necessary in the rural system, the management of which is best done at higher levels.

In addition to the drawbacks of subprovincial fund management, using the one-year deposit rate of interest as the rate of return for individual accounts will likely prove problematic over time (as has been the case for urban schemes). Although very secure, such a low rate virtually guarantees a low individual account balance at retirement and thus weakens participation incentives for rural workers. Even given the appropriate desire to limit investment risk, other approaches, such as notional defined contribution schemes, can in principle address this objective while still providing an adequate rate of return.

The following specific elements of eligibility for the scheme would benefit from being closely monitored and reviewed over time:

- *Retirement age of 60.* For the present, this requirement is sensible in its alignment with the urban scheme. At the same time, the aging of China's population will demand the upward adjustment of retirement ages over time; such adjustment should be considered sooner rather than later by both rural and urban systems. A pressing need exists for reliable—and periodically updated—rural mortality tables to assess the appropriateness of the coefficient of 139 in the drawdown phase of individual account balances. The coefficient is aligned with that used by the urban system but should, in principle, be fine-tuned to line up with rural mortality trends.

- *Policies for vulnerable groups for whom local governments are expected to pay partial or full individual account contributions.* The State Council document leaves this issue open, referring to groups "with paying difficulties . . . like those with serious disabilities" (State Council 2009b). Given the importance of the principle of equity underlying this provision, development of a better-defined common policy for people for whom contributions should be made (and in what amounts) would be useful. Apart from those with disabilities, for example, adults in *dibao* households would appear to be included under this provision. Practice appears quite mixed; some areas contribute on behalf of *dibao* households, in whole or in part, whereas other areas have adopted narrower categories of eligibility.[17] Considering whether the central government should fund—or partly fund—such contributions, perhaps together with local authorities, would also be useful. Although central funding raises the risk that local-level authorities will game the system, that risk could presumably be controlled through clear guidelines on eligible populations and would obviate the risk of excluding poor people in fiscally constrained localities.

- *Eligibility of workers with rural* hukou *who reside in urban areas but are not enrolled in the urban pension system.*[18] In principle, the scheme allows workers with rural *hukou* to participate and to receive local and central subsidies even when residing in cities (a modern-day example of *nong cun bao wei cheng shi*, "the countryside encircling the cities"). In monitoring implementation, attention should be given to see how this element plays out, and the policy interactions with emerging urban residents' pension schemes should be studied. Although the current residence of workers (rather than *hukou*) should, of course, not affect the central subsidy, the incentives are questionable for local authorities to (a) match individual account contributions and (b) supplement the basic pension benefit for workers with local rural *hukou* who do not currently reside in the rural locality.

The policy anticipates but does not clearly address the portability of pension rights under the new scheme. This issue is important and should be addressed soon. Portability of vested rights and individual account balances—both across rural areas and between rural and urban schemes—is important given China's increasingly mobile labor force. The recent document (State Council 2009c) on the portability of rights within the urban enterprise system suggests that the issue has been recognized. Ensuring that portability (both in policy and in practice) in the new rural scheme is aligned with emerging practices in the urban scheme is essential if the new scheme is to achieve its social security and labor market objectives. In practical terms, portability will require the rapid development of systems to reliably transfer information and funds across localities.

The implementation of the scheme will face four key challenges (on which the MHRSS is already focusing):

- *Capacity at local levels, particularly at the county level and below.* The massive and very rapid expansion of the system will place demands on local-level implementation and delivery capacity. These demands will present real challenges in many areas, particularly in service delivery for participants and beneficiaries. The government's intention is to introduce rural social security service centers at least down to (and ideally below) the county level. However, existing staffing ratios imply service loads in an expanding system well above those one would typically observe internationally for similar schemes. At the same time, interesting experiences are emerging from initial partnerships with the banking sector that are helping spread the administrative burden of managing client contributions and basic record keeping (for example, in Ping Yuan County in Guangdong Province).

- *Establishing information systems required to support the new program and linking them to related programs, such as the New Cooperative Medical Scheme, and to other localities.* The government's stated intention is to extend the systems to grassroots levels, although implementation presents challenges for both the systems' capacities and personnel training. Moreover, it risks fragmentation of information systems if not closely managed (although the standardized software from the MHRSS should help in promoting greater coherence than has been observed in urban schemes). The challenge of integrating information systems is likely to be more acute in provinces where management of the New Cooperative Medical Scheme and the new rural pension scheme remains divided between the Ministry of Health and the MHRSS.

- *Penetration of financial and banking services in rural areas and the effect of implementing the scheme on payment systems and the systems of collections for contributions.* The MHRSS is working actively on this issue in cooperation with national banks for better rural coverage (one example of such a partnership is with the Postal Savings Bank), but even banks with extensive coverage do not have branches in all townships (an estimated 7 percent of townships do not yet have a bank). The roles for nonbank financial institutions and reliance on mobile banking may merit further exploration (Pickens, Porteous, and Rotman 2009).

- *The level of contribution matching for individual accounts across counties (which raises issues of equity).* The obvious challenge is avoiding a situation in which poor counties fail to match individual account contributions (resulting in lower accumulations for the poor) while still maintaining enough local interest in the scheme to encourage accountability at the county level. Initial experience suggests that different balances are being struck. In some provinces (for example, Mongolia and Ningxia), the province has been financing the match, whereas in others (for example, Shandong), the aim is to have the counties entirely finance the match.

As stated earlier, the new rural pension pilot has many positive and innovative features. At the same time, although the scheme relies on a broadly sensible design and represents a milestone in social policy in China, the preceding discussion of issues identifies scope for improvement and further refinement of some policy parameters if China's objectives are to be fully attained.

In addition to the new rural pension pilot, experience is growing with "urban resident" pension schemes, designed along similar lines to the rural pension pilot. The potential dovetailing of these schemes and those for rural workers over time is another emerging issue in pension policy. In cities with sufficient fiscal capacity, a recent rapid expansion in local schemes offers residents outside the urban workers' scheme a combination of an individual account and a basic pension. In some cases (for example, Hangzhou), local authorities match individual account contributions, whereas in others (for example, Beijing), no such match occurs. In rapidly expanding areas, such schemes have already been merged with ongoing rural schemes to achieve an integrated residents' pension scheme;

in a number of cases, benefit levels are equivalent between participants with urban *hukou* and those with rural *hukou* from the prefecture. Like the rural pension pilot, such initiatives seem promising as vehicles for expanding pension coverage to the nonwage sector and for promoting the vision laid out by policy makers of rural-urban integration.

Conclusion

The experience reviewed in this chapter suggests a number of areas that will require particular attention from national policy makers as they implement the national pilot and continue to develop the national policy framework for rural pensions. These areas include (a) the appropriate split between the central government and subnational levels on financing roles; (b) portfolio rules and balancing protection of pension investments against the need for adequate returns to increase the real value of pensions; (c) issues of regulation and oversight that continue to remain weak; (d) treatment of the population over 45 years of age, who will have insufficient contribution histories under regular rules; (e) a close examination of appropriate retirement ages based on updated rural mortality information; (f) transition and portability issues between old rural schemes and new schemes, and between rural and urban schemes; and (g) specific financing options, such as buffer funds, to deal with an aging rural population.

The next chapter considers possible directions for evolution of the national rural pension pilot in the medium term, acknowledging the many positive features of the pilot. As discussed in this chapter, the national pilot is a milestone in the development of the rural social protection system in China. As it is rolled out, review of whether further refinements are desirable, in particular those related to universality of coverage of the basic benefit and the relative incentive roles of the individual account and the basic benefits, will be useful. The following chapter discusses these issues, offering proposals for consideration.

Notes

1. In October 1995, the State Council redistributed a MOCA circular, "Further Improving the Rural Pension Insurance."

2. The pension benefit calculation formula was $(0.008631526) *$ (accumulation in individual account).

3. See P. Chen (2002), Liang (1999), Ma (1999), and Shi (2006) for a discussion of the shortcomings of previous rural pension schemes.

4. See Peng (1996) for examples of massive differences in the matching of cadre and farmer contributions under local schemes.

5. For detailed descriptions of the systems of Baoji, Beijing, Suzhou, and Yantai, see Wu (2009). For a detailed discussion of the Baoji pilot rural pension experience, see Zhang and Dan (2008).

6. See Zhang and Dan (2008), who argue that such a system will encourage family disputes, whereas Sun (2006) considers such a system to be a pragmatic and innovative approach to addressing individuals with short contribution histories.

7. For a comprehensive discussion of recent experiences with "closing the coverage gap" through the extension of pension systems to rural and informal sector populations, see Holzmann, Robalino, and Takayama (2009); see Palacios and Robalino (2009) on the framework for matching defined contribution schemes.

8. See Lin (2006) for European, Commonwealth of Independent States, and low-income countries; Gong (2006) for Japan; Su (2007) for the Republic of Korea; and Leisering, Sen, and Hussain (2002) and Zheng (2007) for a general discussion of the subsidy approach.

9. See Zhuhai City, "Transitional Pension Method for Farmers and Land-Expropriated Farmers," as described by Wu (2009). Along similar lines, Donghua Wang (2006) has suggested that income from the auction of land-use rights and resources from state-owned assets should also be used for such purposes.

10. See Y. Chen (2004) and Dong (2008). The assumptions underlying these simulations merit note. For example, Chen used a projection model based on data from Jiangsu Province and assumes that one-quarter of the increase in general revenues would be needed for rural pension subsidies to support a universal pension for men and women at age 60 and 55, respectively. Assuming this subsidy represents 2.5 percent of general revenues, a universal farmers' pension of 825 yuan annually could have been provided in 2010.

11. See Y. Chen (2004) and Qin (2007) for approaches to allocating financing responsibility among levels.

12. See Mi and Yang (2008) on the grain payment proposal, supported by a survey in Anhui Province that found that about one-fifth of rural respondents would prefer to make contributions in grain. See Lu (2004) and Zhan (2004) for proposals for the allocation of grain subsidies to farmers.

13. See L. Zhang (2007) regarding a reserve fund proposal. See Lü (2005) for proposals for higher-return portfolio options.

14. See http://www.cnr.cn/china/gdgg/201009/t20100907_507012375.html.

15. See World Bank (forthcoming b) for a discussion of social assistance benefits in rural areas. Roughly 5.3 million people received *wubao* nationwide in 2007.

16. Chile provides an example of such an approach.

17. The possible coverage of *dibao* household contributions raises secondary questions about how to subsequently treat rural pension income in the *dibao* eligibility determination process, because the marginal cost of pension receipts could easily outweigh benefits once both the loss of the *dibao* benefits and the attendant noncash benefits that attach to *dibao* receipt are taken into account.

18. *Hukou* is the residence permit system in China, which assigns the permit largely according to place of birth and the residence status of one's parents.

References

Beijing Municipal Government. 2005. "Notice of Guide on Construction of Rural Social Pension of Beijing Government." [In Chinese.] Accessed October 12, 2011. http://govfile.beijing.gov.cn/Govfile/front/content/22005062_0.html.

———. 2007. "Provisional Method for New Rural Social Pension." [In Chinese.] Accessed October 12, 2011. http://zhengwu.beijing.gov.cn/fggz/zfgz/t932987.htm.

———. 2009. "New Pension Scheme for Both Rural and Urban Residents." [In Chinese.] Accessed October 12, 2011. http://zhengwu.beijing.gov.cn/gzdt/gggs/t1015867.htm.

Chen, Ping. 2002. "Establishing a Unified Social Security System Is a Shortsighted Policy." [In Chinese.] *China Reform* 4: 16–17.

Chen, Yi. 2004. "Rural Pension: Design and Argument for a New Scheme." [In Chinese.] *Academic World* 5.

Dong, Keyong. 2008. "Establishing a Universal Pension Scheme in Rural Areas." China Youth News, July 16, 2008.

Gong, Xiaoxia. 2006. "Rural Pension System and Its Lessons in Developed Countries." [In Chinese.] *Journal of Central Finance University* 6.

Holzmann, Robert, David Robalino, and Noriuki Takayama, eds. 2009. *Closing the Coverage Gap: Role of Social Pensions and Other Retirement Income Transfers.* Washington, DC: World Bank.

Leisering, Lutz, Gong Sen, and Athar Hussain. 2002. *People's Republic of China: Old-Age Pensions for the Rural Areas: From Land Reform to Globalization.* Manila, Philippines: Asian Development Bank.

Liang, Hong. 1999. "Economic Analysis of Current Rural Community Security of China." [In Chinese.] Dissertation, University of Fudan.

Lin, Yi. 2006. *Research on International Comparison of Rural Social Security and Its Lessons.* [In Chinese.] Beijing: China Labor and Social Security Publishing House.

Liu, Chunzhi. 2007. "Improving Rural Pension Scheme Design." [In Chinese.] *China Finance* 6.

Liu, Zilan. 2008. "Reflection and Reconstruction of China Rural Pension." [In Chinese.] *Business School of Hu'an Normal University, Management World* 8: 46–56.

Lu, Haiyuan. 2004. "Innovation of Rural Social Pension Scheme: Produce for Social Security." [In Chinese.] *Seeking Truth* 3.

Lü, Jiming. 2005. "Current Situation of Rural Social Security and Analysis of Its Development Path." [In Chinese.] *Journal of Ningxia Communist School* 6. http://en.cnki.com.cn/Article_en/CJFDTOTAL-NXDB200506013.htm.

Ma, Limin. 1999. "Slowing Down Rural Pension." [In Chinese.] *Exploration and Debate* 7: 11–12.

Mi, Hong, and Cuiying Yang. 2008. *Basic Theoretic Framework Research on Rural Pension System.* [In Chinese.] Guang Ming Publishing House, Shanghai.

MOCA (Ministry of Civil Affairs). 1993–97. Bulletins. Ministry of Civil Afairs, Beijing.

———. 1995. "Further Improving the Rural Pension Insurance." [In Chinese.] Accessed October 12, 2011. http://gd.lss.gov.cn/gdlss/zcfg/zc/ncshbx/ncylxgl/t19951019_3337.htm.

MOLSS (Ministry of Labor and Social Security). 1998–2007. Bulletins. Beijing, MOLSS.

———. 2003. "Notice on Seriously Improving Work on Current Rural Pensions." [In Chinese.] Accessed October12, 2011. http://jlfusong.si.gov.cn/E_ReadNews.asp?NewsID=139.

NBS (National Bureau of Statistics). 2009. *Chinese Labor and Social Security Yearbook 2008.* Beijing: Chinese Labor and Social Security Yearbook Editorial.

———. 2008. *Chinese Labor and Social Security Yearbook 2007.* Beijing: Chinese Labor and Social Security Yearbook Editorial.

———. 2007. *Chinese Labor and Social Security Yearbook 2006.* Beijing: Chinese Labor and Social Security Yearbook Editorial.

———. 2006. *Chinese Labor and Social Security Yearbook 2005.* Beijing: Chinese Labor and Social Security Yearbook Editorial.

———. 2005. *Chinese Labor and Social Security Yearbook 2004.* Beijing: Chinese Labor and Social Security Yearbook Editorial.

———. 2004. *Chinese Labor and Social Security Yearbook 2003.* Beijing: Chinese Labor and Social Security Yearbook Editorial.

———. 2003. *Chinese Labor and Social Security Yearbook 2002.* Beijing: Chinese Labor and Social Security Yearbook Editorial.

———. 2002. *Chinese Labor and Social Security Yearbook 2001.* Beijing: Chinese Labor and Social Security Yearbook Editorial.

Palacios, Robert, and David Robalino. 2009. "Matching Defined Contributions: A Way to Increase Pension Coverage." In *Closing the Coverage Gap: The Role of Social Pensions and Other Retirement Income Transfers*, ed. Robert Holzmann, David Robalino, and Noriyuki Takayama, 187–202. Washington, DC: World Bank.

Peng, Xisheng. 1996. "Township and Village Enterprises and Rural Social Security in the South of Jiangsu Province." [In Chinese.] *Shanghai Finance* 6: 31–32.

Pickens, Mark, David Porteous, and Sarah Rotman. 2009. "Banking the Poor via G2P Payments." *Focus Note* 58. Washington, DC: CGAP.

Qin, Zhongchun. 2007. "The Urgency, Current Situation and Policy Recommendation on Building Rural Pension System." [In Chinese.] *China Economic Times*.

Shi, Shih-Jiunn. 2006. "Left to Market and Family—Again? Ideas and the Development of the Rural Pension Policy in China." *Social Policy and Administration* 40 (7): 791–806.

State Council. 1986. "The 7th Five-Year Plan for National Economic and Social Development of the People's Republic of China, 1986–1990." [In Chinese.] Beijing: People's Publishing House.

———. 1991. "Decision on Establishing a Unified Basic Old Age Insurance for Enterprise Employees." Document 33. [In Chinese.] Accessed in October 12, 2011. http://csi001.zj001.net/show_hdr.php?xname=NI921V0&dname=6V065V0&xpos=1.

———. 2009a. "Achieving Steady Agricultural Development and Sustained Income Increases for Farmers." Document 1 [In Chinese.] Accessed October 5, 2011. http://www.gov.cn/jrzg/2009-02/01/content_1218759.htm.

———. 2009b. "Guiding Suggestions of the State Council on Developing New Rural Pension Scheme Pilot." Document 32 [In Chinese.] Accessed October 12, 2011 http://www.gov.cn/xxgk/pub/govpublic/mrlm/200909/t20090904_33900.html?keywords=.

———. 2009c. "Interim Provisions on the Portability of Pension Benefits of Urban Enterprise Pension System." Circular of the General Office of the State Council issued jointly by the Ministry of Human Resources and Social Security and Ministry of Finance. Document No. 66. General Office of the State Council, Beijing.

———. 2011. "Twelfth Five-Year Plan." [In Chinese.] Beijing: People's Publishing House.

Su, Baozhong. 2007. "Rural Pension Systems of Western Developed Countries and Its Lessons." [In Chinese.] *Current Economy* 12.

Suzhou Municipal Government. 2003. "Provisional Methods for Rural Pension." Accessed October 12, 2011. http://www.law-lib.com/law/law_view.asp?id=74738.

Sun, Wenji. 2006. *Building and Perfecting the Institution of Social Security in Rural Areas*. [In Chinese.] Beijing: Social Science Academic Press.

Wang, Donghua. 2006. "Construction of Pension System in Context of Coordinating Rural and Urban Development." [In Chinese.] *Theoretic Frontier* 15.

Wang, Guojun. 2000. "Defects of Current Rural Pension System and Reform Thinking." [In Chinese.] *Quarterly of Shanghai Academy of Social Science* 1: 120–27.

Wang, Zhengqiong. 2004. "Preliminary Study on Rural Pension System." [In Chinese.] *Enterprises Economy* 9.

World Bank. Forthcoming a. *China: A Vision for Pension Policy Reform Options.* Washington, DC: World Bank.

———. Forthcoming b. *Social Assistance in Rural China: Tackling Poverty through Rural Dibao*. Washington, DC: World Bank.

Wu, Yuning. 2009. "Literature Review of China Rural Pension System." Background paper prepared for World Bank East Asia Social Protection Unit, Beijing.

Yang, Cuiying. 2007. *Nong cun ji ben yang lao bao xian zhi du li lun yu zheng ce yan jiu.* [Studies on rural social pension insurance system in China: Practice, theory, and policy]. Hangzhou: Zhejiang da xue chu ban she.

Yang, Jainguo. 2007. "Innovation and Selection of Financing Sources of Rural Social Security" [In Chinese.] *Development Research* 2.

Yang, Jainguo 2007. "Innovation and Selection of Financing Sources of Rural Social Security." Developing Research 2007 (2).

Yantai Municipal Government. 2007. "Provisional Method on New Rural Pension Insurance." *Accessed October 12, 2011. http://ld.yantai.gov.cn/img/%E3%80% 8A%E7%83%9F%E5%8F%B0%E5%B8%82%E6%96%B0%E5%9E%8B%E5% 86%9C%E6%9D%91%E7%A4%BE%E4%BC%9A%E5%85%BB%E8%80% 81%E4%BF%9D%E9%99%A9%E6%9A%82%E8%A1%8C%E5%8A%9E%E6 %B3%95%E3%80%8B.pdf.*

Zhan, Zhongqing. 2004. "Feasibility Analysis of Utilizing Grain Subsidy to Build Rural Social Security." [In Chinese.] *Survey World* 2.

Zhang, Lingjun. 2006. "Issues of Rural Pension Fund Management and Its Policy Recommendation." [In Chinese.] *Rural Finance and Accounting* 7.

Zhang, Wenjuan, and Tang Dan. 2008. "The New Rural Social Pension Insurance Programme of Baoji City." Chiang Mai, Thailand: HelpAge International–Asia/Pacific. www.helpage.org/download/4c48ab08674c1/.

Zheng, Wei. 2007. "Reflection on the Dilemma of China Rural Pension System." [In Chinese.] *Insurance Research* 11.

CHAPTER 6

Issues for the Evolution of the Rural Pension System

Building on the national rural pension pilot, this chapter outlines issues for further development of the rural pension system over the medium term. As noted in the previous chapter, the national pension pilot is an exciting and positive development in expanding pension coverage to the rural population. At the same time, as the system evolves, opportunities for further adjustments in policy may arise to realize the government's objectives over the longer term. This chapter lays out ideas as well as relevant international experience for Chinese policy makers to consider as they continue to refine the rural pension system.[1] Several key issues are addressed:

- The appropriate level of the matching subsidy on individual accounts and its role relative to the basic pension benefit with regard to incentives to participate in the scheme
- Individual account contributions and options for reducing the problem of low rates of return that have been seen in the urban funded system
- Whether the basic pension benefit in the national pilot should in time evolve into a "social pension" in which coverage does not depend on contributions

- The interaction between the funded portion of the rural pension system and the basic benefit in the longer term
- Prospects for eventual integration of rural pensions and urban "residents' pension" schemes

Pension System Design Principles

Both in China and internationally, general agreement exists that an effective and sustainable pension scheme should have the following attributes:

- *Adequacy*. The benefit levels provided should be sufficient to perform the most basic function of promoting security in old age.
- *Breadth*. The system should provide basic protection to the vast majority of workers and retirees (that is, it should have broad coverage), offering the possibility of saving for retirement and life-cycle consumption smoothing, including individuals without stable income.
- *Sustainability*. The system design needs to be robust in the face of shocks and demographic trends (the latter is of special concern in China, as was noted earlier).
- *Affordability*. The government, individuals, and employers should be able to afford the system, both in a strict financial sense and, more broadly, at a level that does not inhibit labor market efficiency and the economic competitiveness of enterprises.
- *Multiple layers*. Although perhaps not as axiomatic as the preceding principles, international experience strongly points to the benefits of diversification of risks during the accumulation and decumulation phases of a pension system, thereby contributing to benefit predictability.

Issues Regarding the Individual Account

The Matching Subsidy

Offering a matching subsidy in the national scheme represents a major shift and recognition by authorities that incentives are needed to attract the participation of rural populations (a lesson that also has relevance for urban nonwage populations). The policy direction is also consistent with experience in many member countries of the Organisation for Economic Co-operation and Development (OECD) and in a number of middle-income countries, such as Brazil and Mexico, as discussed later in this chapter.[2] The Chinese literature has addressed the need for incentives, and the move toward public subsidies for rural pensions has generally been supported.[3]

Determining the appropriate matching rate by the public sector (and hence the fiscal cost of the match) is not straightforward; the performance of the new scheme should be closely monitored to select the most appropriate match. This determination will depend on several factors, including available resources, the elasticity of take-up against different rates of matching (see below for an illustration of this relationship), and the interaction of the contributory system with other forms of public transfers for the elderly. Despite widespread matching for fully funded pension schemes, virtually no robust evidence exists to relate matching rates with participation rates. Too low a match will create an insufficient incentive for participation. Too high a match will create a large fiscal burden and is poorly targeted with regard to poverty alleviation because everyone will benefit from the match, including those who are comparatively well-off. A related question is whether the match should vary as a function of the level of individual contributions or should be flat, perhaps based on some share of average rural income or urban wages in the area. This may invoke a trade-off between equity and fiscal concerns on one hand and the relative strength of incentives to contribute more than the minimum rate on the other. The evidence on saving behavior in China suggests that concerns about incentivizing saving for retirement may be less acute than they are in many countries, thus strengthening the justification for focusing on the lower end of the distribution.

Although no strong evidence exists to suggest an optimal matching defined contribution (MDC) matching rate, simulations are instructive. Palacios and Robalino (2009) estimate that an MDC approach can be cost-effective provided that (a) the take-up rate matching elasticity is not too low (below approximately 0.15) and (b) the individual contribution rates are not too low (below approximately 5 percent of average earnings). Overall, the study posits that (a) matching rates that are too low could cost more in the long run than do social pensions and that (b) "too low" could be below 0.50 or even one to one (Palacios and Robalino 2009). These findings must be interpreted with caution, however, because much of the evidence on matching comes from voluntary urban enterprise occupational schemes and the 401(k) experience in the United States (see figure 6.1). However, the findings raise questions about whether the current level of matching in the national rural pension pilot will be sufficient to sustain incentives for younger workers to participate.

Figure 6.1   Take-up Rate and Matching Contributions

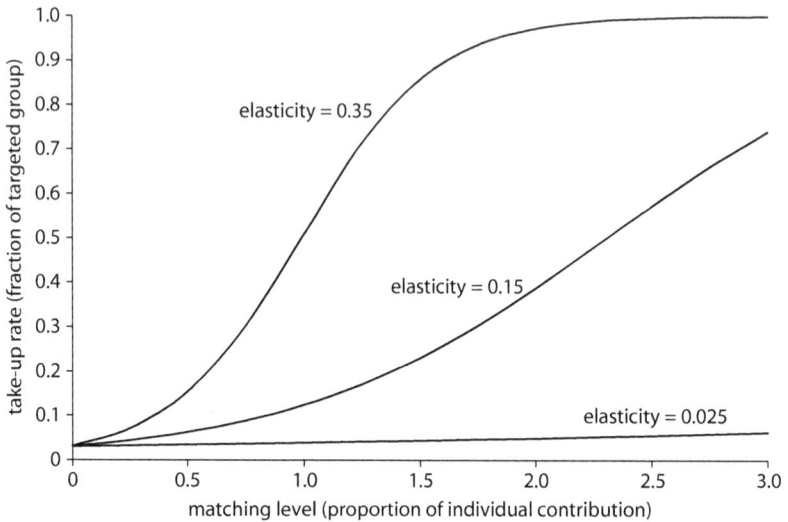

Source: Palacios and Robalino 2009.
Note: The take-up rate is defined by $TR = exp(z)/(1 - exp(z))$ where $z = -3.45 + b*(0.05*m)/0.5$, where $b/100$ is the take-up rate matching elasticity and m is the level of matching. In this example, 0.05 refers to the contribution rate expressed as a share of average earnings and 0.5 is the income of the plan member relative to average earnings. The parameter -3.45 was calibrated to reproduce a take-up rate of 3 percent when $m = 0$.

Apart from the total amount (or rate) of the match, a clear decision should be made on which level of the system should fund matching contributions for individual accounts. From an equity standpoint—and, in insurance terms, to promote a higher level of risk pool—the higher in the system the match's source, the better. However, this decision must be balanced against both the practicalities of matching in an environment in which contributions will vary across and within provinces (and hence potentially complex for the national government to determine the matching funds or to demand a flat match that would result in variable incentives across space) and the objectives of the central government that may place more weight on the flat portion of a future scheme. In this light, the recommendation is that matching funds come from the provincial level or below, or possibly some mix of the two, with the province providing a "floor match" of some agreed-on flat amount and localities supplementing it if they are able and willing.

Another important question is whether to mandate that employers and collectives contribute to matching individual contributions in cases in which such an employment relationship exists. Although such contributions may well be desirable in principle—and would provide closer parallels with the urban worker pension scheme—experience of previous rural schemes suggests that such a requirement may not be realistic.[4] The rural pension pilot allows such contributions but does not rely on them to the degree that some schemes have in the past.

Investment and Management of Individual Accounts

The rules governing the investment of accumulations will have important repercussions for the level of income replacement the individual account will provide. Experience thus far with rural and urban pension schemes in China suggests that investment of accumulations is a key vulnerability in a scheme's ability to provide adequate benefits at retirement. At this point, an appropriate governance and investment management framework for rural or urban residents' pensions is lacking. Low and volatile returns on contributions in rural pension schemes have been one of their greatest weaknesses to date, a vulnerability shared by China's funded urban schemes. The People's Bank of China requires investments to be made in one-year time deposits, which have generated low real returns over the past decade (on the order of 1–2 percent annually in the urban individual account system), far less than both rural and urban income growth. At the same time, policy makers are understandably reluctant to expose rural and urban nonwage populations to significant investment risk, given their general lack of financial sophistication and the underdeveloped state of governance.

The key determinant of the real value of the individual account portion of the pension will be the rate of return earned on contributions during the accumulation phase. Figure 6.2 presents a simulation of the benefit level from an individual account based on a total annual contribution of 360 renminbi (RMB) in present-value terms (that is, just under three times the current minimum combined contribution from the individual plus a government match) and based on the following assumptions: (a) the scheme is launched in 2010, (b) rural mortality remains unchanged, (c) the retirement age is increased to 65, (d) benefits are price indexed, (e) the real discount rate is 2.5 percent, and (f) the wedge between real rate of return and real wage growth is −1.0 percent over the first 10 years and 1.0 percent afterward. Figure 6.2 shows the relatively modest individual account accumulation that will likely result under this set of plausible assumptions with a retirement age that is notably higher than that currently adopted in the national rural pension pilot. Of course, the national pilot's total replacement rate will not be based

Figure 6.2   Present Value of Individual Account Monthly Benefit by Years of Contributions Given a 360 RMB Total Annual Contribution

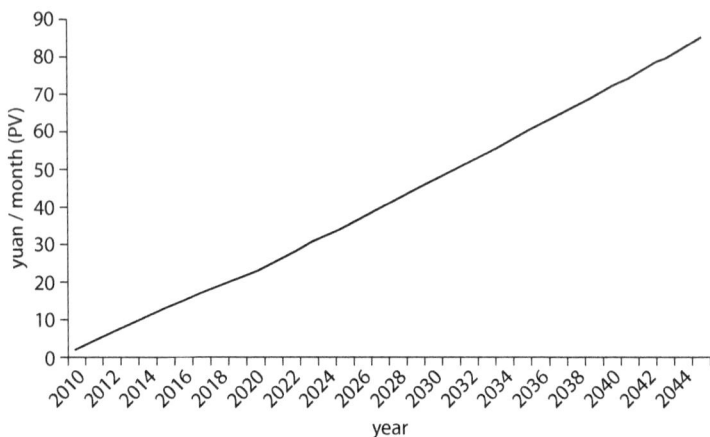

Source: World Bank forthcoming.
Note: Assumes (a) current rural mortality; (b) price indexation; (c) retirement age of 65; (d) real discount rate of 2.5 percent; (e) the wedge between real rate of return and real wage growth is −1.0 percent over the first 10 years and 1.0 percent afterward; and (f) the scheme begins in 2010. PV = present value.

solely on benefits paid from individual accounts. But the example underscores the importance of ongoing consideration of the *total replacement rates* the authorities will seek from their rural pilot and urban residents' schemes and the contribution toward the level of income replacement that can realistically be expected from individual accounts under the current minimum required contributions and government match.

An alternative—and, in the view of this book, preferred—approach would be for the central government to provide a guaranteed rate of return on the individual accounts. The guaranteed rate of return could be set at the national growth rate of the gross domestic product (GDP). This approach would offer a workable compromise between the competing objectives of security and adequacy of returns.

Although it may be too complicated at this stage, an option for the future would be to allow different investment rules for different cohorts of workers participating in the individual account scheme. For older workers, having conservative investment rules makes sense because it limits exposure to market risk and volatility and takes account of their lower degree of financial literacy. However, for younger workers, the compounded effects of rules for low rates of return on conservative investments are likely to be large, and their extended contribution histories will allow for averaging market volatility across the life cycle. The authorities might consider using age-based portfolio default rules, which allow more aggressive investment for younger contributors that gradually becomes more conservative over the life cycle to focus on preserving the value of accumulations at retirement.

Another question that merits consideration is whether a reserve fund is desirable. The answer depends in part on the intended long-term role of the basic pension benefit and any future social pension for the elderly. Such funds are more typically used to address fluctuations in returns or the exhaustion of benefits because of longevity. In principle, the concept of a reserve fund is attractive, and practice in places such as Zhuhai indicates interest.[5]

Management of funds in individual accounts and the appropriate level of the system for management also merit consideration. Current pilot schemes and past practice have generally involved management at the county level. However, combining funds from localities into a single pool that can be managed at higher levels to generate economies of scale in fund management has clear benefits. China's experience with rural pensions cautions against localized management and investment of accumulations. A sensible option would be to have the National Social Security Fund (NSSF) manage funds in rural individual accounts, although considerable preparation would be required for the infrastructure to record and remit balances to the NSSF and to make transfers back to paying authorities as the system matures. More specifically, the new scheme could put the public subsidy for individual accounts into the NSSF and put contributions in the Agricultural Bank of China, the Postal Savings Bank, or other suitable financial institutions, with a uniform interest rate announced nationally and recorded in individual account passbooks. Although the option of contracting fund management to authorized asset managers might be considered in the longer run, it would require a much stronger regulatory and accountability framework than exists presently.[6]

With respect to the regulation of funded rural pension schemes, capacity is presently inadequate; lack of capacity has been an ongoing weakness of rural schemes in China (see World Bank forthcoming; Wu 2009). In addition, existing capacity to regulate even urban schemes is stretched. Thus, rather than creating new institutions for regulating funded rural pensions, strengthening capacity in existing urban institutions to expand coverage to rural areas would seem more desirable. Taking such an approach would also help achieve critical mass in regulatory capacity.

For the credibility and utility of the individual account in the medium term, permitting account holders to borrow a portion of their account accumulations at a specified interest rate and with legally binding repayment conditions is probably desirable. Eligible conditions might include the purchase of a home, certain types of health care costs, or costs for children's education. In some systems, including 401(k) accounts in the United States, such "borrowings" are repaid at a designated interest rate by the individual. In other schemes, loans simply reduce the total accumulated balance. Given the volatility of nonwage incomes and the economic conditions of residents who work outside the formal sector, the opportunity to borrow from one's individual accounts would be an attractive feature of the scheme; the structure of such a feature should be considered, ensuring, of course, that an adequate minimum accumulation will be available at retirement.

Rules for payouts must be developed. The options include annuitization, phased withdrawal, and lump-sum payouts. Previous rural schemes have used phased withdrawal, which would be adequate for the foreseeable future, but authorities should look toward eventually providing annuities instead. The lump-sum option, however, will likely be important for the transitional generation (which is discussed further below). Some previous rural schemes in China provided for the lump-sum repayment of contributions to those without full contribution histories. In some cases, repayment was made at the point of retirement (for example, in Beijing and Zhuhai); in others, repayment was made during the accumulation phase. Other schemes have given older cohorts the option of continuing to contribute for up to five years after reaching the normal retirement age.

Notional or Fully Funded Accounts for the Individual Account?

A bigger-picture question on the individual account portion of the rural pension scheme is whether the funding of public subsidies for individual accounts should be actual or notional.[7] If investment of accumulations is restricted to bank deposits at fixed interest rates—which has been the case in urban schemes and most rural pilots to date—the more fundamental question is whether funded individual accounts or notional defined contribution (NDC) accounts are the preferred approach. The relative attraction of actual versus notional funding depends on a few key factors. The first is the investment rules for the individual account (including consideration of possible guarantees for rates of return), which were discussed earlier. If investments are constrained to fixed-interest deposits in public sector banks, the effective difference between funded schemes and NDC schemes is significantly reduced. Second, the policy choices for the future of the urban system may be relevant, given the government's desire for greater harmonization of urban and rural pension systems over time. If the urban system moves to an NDC design at some point, the attraction of notional funding for subsidies on individual accounts for the rural scheme increases. Counterbalancing these factors, however, are two significant issues that are specific to rural individual accounts. First, farmers lack awareness of the NDC concept and have a natural skepticism toward past scheme performance based on the promises of rural pension schemes that are not funded—"real money" would be a more intuitive concept for farmers. Second, and even more important from a structural viewpoint, the demographic transition in rural areas in the coming decades would argue against an NDC approach. On balance, therefore, pursuing a fully funded approach to the individual account, as is being done under the national pilot scheme, makes sense.

Portability between Schemes

Transition issues will become important as the national rural pension scheme matures. The first type of transition is from old to new rural pension schemes within the same locality. Practice in China has varied, with areas such as Beijing allowing portability of funded accumulations from old to new schemes, whereas others, such as the province of Hunan, stipulate that participants must close their accounts in old schemes before starting afresh in new pilots.[8] The national scheme appears to allow transfers of balances from prior schemes. The second (and ultimately more important) issue is portability between rural and urban schemes (or migrant-worker schemes located in urban areas where they exist). Portability will be critical to reaching the government's stated goal of an integrated social security system by 2020. The ease of portability has varied according to scheme design and the compatibility of rural pilots with existing urban schemes. Suzhou, for example, has had a simple two-to-one rule for farmers wishing to transfer their social pooling rights from the rural to the urban scheme; transfer is easily done because the rural contribution base has been exactly half that of the urban system. Beijing has also had provisions for portability, although it occurs only at the point of retirement. If a former farmer has accumulated enough years in the urban system at retirement, he or she will enjoy an urban pension (with an allowance for lower rural contributions), whereas his or her urban contributions will be credited to the rural pension scheme if the accumulation period in the urban system is fewer than 15 years. In principle, in all schemes, the funded portion can easily become portable. Because the MDC design adopted in the national rural pilot has no social pooling, apportionment is not an issue.

Having a funded portion in the rural pension system may be useful for rural workers who move either to other rural areas without *hukou* or to urban areas. In principle, transferring balances from one scheme to another in the funded portion through totalization agreements between schemes should be straightforward. This approach raises the question, however, of whether to also consider pooling urban and rural accumulations in the provinces and combining fund management. Such an approach has merit, although it may require greater coordination than is possible in the short run.

The issue of portability raises a host of design and implementation questions that will need to be closely considered during the pilot phase of the rural pension system. When a worker moves, will the funds in his or her account move or will only his or her contribution records move? How will the system account for accumulations in the rural system when workers move to the urban system? Finally, are pensions paid from various locations or from a single payment authority? These sorts of practical questions raise issues for record keeping, communication and information exchange between systems, and exchange of account information. In principle, standardized record-keeping and reporting formats for the new rural pension system (which have been developed and are being disseminated by the Ministry of Human Resources and Social Security) should be capable of addressing such practical questions. The harmonization of fund transfer and pension disbursement procedures would also be required. Again, some degree of centralization would be desirable to lessen administrative demands at the lower levels, although centralization might occur at the provincial level within national guidelines. These issues will require elaborated guidance from the central authorities over time.

International Experience with MDCs[9]
The MDC approach is relatively new but is being explored in a number of developing countries. Many OECD countries provide tax incentives to encourage workers and employers to contribute to voluntary private pension schemes. Most OECD countries provide incentives of at least 10 percent of contributions—the average is around 20 percent—although this provision is made through tax deductions for employers on such

contributions (Yoo and de Serres 2004). In the United States, for example, the value of forgone tax revenue for such deductions is equivalent to 1 percent of GDP. Evidence shows that such programs increase participation, although the composition of savings is affected rather than its overall level. What seems clearer is that tax exemptions increase saving among low-income people and others with low saving rates (Benjamin 2003; Engen and Gale 2000). However, given progressive tax scales in most OECD countries, subsidies tend to benefit better-off workers disproportionately in absolute terms. In any event, using tax exemptions to subsidize pension contributions would likely prove less effective in developing countries, where the poor are less likely to be subject to taxes in the first place and where distributional concerns on the use of public subsidies may be more pressing. In China, a tax exemption would be meaningless for the large majority of rural workers because their incomes are below the minimum personal income tax threshold. Because the majority of rural workers do not pay income tax, the direct match approach is preferred. That option is precisely the one chosen by the Chinese authorities in the national pilot, and it seems appropriate.

Experience with MDCs in developing countries is limited. Legislation introducing MDC schemes has been passed in the Dominican Republic, Indonesia, and Vietnam, but they have not yet been implemented. A noteworthy example comes from the Indian states of Rajasthan and Madhya Pradesh, both of which have MDC pension schemes for certain categories of informal sector workers. The schemes provide a one-to-one match on contributions from the state governments. Funds are invested by contracted asset managers with no guaranteed rate of return for contributors. The state of Andhra Pradesh started a similar scheme in 2009 that targeted women in self-help groups, with a subsidy of about US$10 per year per person, which is expected to produce a pension just above the poverty line. The oldest such MDC scheme in India is in West Bengal, which has provided a one-to-one match for roughly 60 categories of informal sector workers since the early 2000s. The Indian government is considering an MDC approach for informal workers on a nationwide basis under its new pension scheme (see box 6.1).

As is the case for all defined contribution schemes, the design of MDCs needs to address two policy issues: (a) how to handle the death or disability of contributors, and (b) how to manage financial risk for contributors (particularly those with low financial literacy). With respect to the former, pure defined contribution schemes do not, by construction, provide insurance against premature death or disability during the

Box 6.1

Rajasthan's Vishwakarma MDC Pension Scheme

In 2007, the government of Rajasthan, India, introduced an MDC scheme for 20 categories of low-income workers, almost all of whom are in the informal sector. To be eligible, workers must (a) be residents of Rajasthan, (b) be between 18 and 50 years of age, and (c) not be covered by any other provident fund arrangement supported by the government or an employer. If workers contribute 100 Indian rupees (just over US$2) per month for at least 10 months each year, the state government will finance a 1,000-rupee annual match on their contribution. An annual interest rate is paid on the combined accumulation; the interest rate is announced each year and is equivalent to the rate of return on the formal sector provident fund (about 8 percent per year in 2008). This computation has been designed to provide a benefit at retirement just above the poverty line. At current interest rates, a 30-year-old worker who contributes for 30 years would receive a monthly pension of about 2,000 rupees at retirement at age 60. The scheme does not allow early withdrawals of accumulations. Account holders are provided an annual account statement. Web-based individual accounts are opened for each worker in the scheme, and a computer-generated passbook is provided within 30 days, which contains a scanned photograph and the enrollment form of the account holder. The individual receives a unique identifier at the point of registration, using an application called the Social Security Solution (sCube), which allows portability of the account and permits the worker to make contributions at any location in the state. Using a variety of options, sCube allows online and offline data entry and requires only a half day of training to operate. Raising the awareness of members is strongly emphasized before and following enrollment, using short films, comics, interactive pension calculators, and other approaches.

Source: Invest India Micro Pension Services Pvt., Ltd., http://www.iimp.in.

accumulation phase. As a result, group life and disability insurance policies are common for contributors in the scheme. Such policies would cover the difference between the individual's account accumulation at the point of death or disability and the benefits paid under the policy in the event of death or disability. The premium is calculated using actuarial statistics for the group. Managing financial risk is handled differently in different countries, ranging from imposing conservative portfolio rules (which is the case in China now) to guaranteeing rates of return to transferring all risk to contributors (which is the case in the Indian schemes previously described). Given the likely degree of risk aversion on the part of rural workers in China and the country's underdeveloped regulatory framework, offering a guaranteed rate of return, as suggested above, seems to be the preferred option for the medium term.

Could the Basic Rural Pension Benefit Evolve into a Social Pension?

A key policy question for the future development of the rural pension system is whether the basic benefit should in time evolve into a "social pension" for which eligibility is not linked to contributions to an individual account, as happens now. International experience reviewed later in this section suggests that full pension coverage is very difficult to achieve at the level of the individual in rural and informal sector schemes based on approaches that require contributions, even with incentives to contribute.

The objective of a social pension would be to ensure basic subsistence for those elderly who are not covered by existing pension provisions or who are unable to generate adequate retirement income from their contributions during their working age. An inability to generate adequate retirement income could occur for a variety of reasons, including sickness, disability, or time out of the workforce (for child rearing, study, and so on). The rationale for a social pension is twofold: (a) to provide a low level of support for the growing number of elderly with minimal resources to prevent them from falling into poverty in their old age, and (b) to reduce incentives for overly high precautionary saving before retirement.

A social pension could follow uniform design parameters nationwide, although benefits would reflect local characteristics. Provincial authorities would be held accountable for observing the national framework. The benefit amount could be set as a percentage of the regional average wage, with the objective of exceeding the per capita benefit under the existing *dibao* scheme. A "pension test" could also reduce the benefit by a proportion of the benefits received from other pension arrangements, say for those 65 to 74 years of age. The pension test would need to be designed to reward those who contributed to other pension schemes while targeting those with the least income from all sources, including other pension benefits. Given the need to eventually increase the retirement age to 65 for men and women, setting 65 as the minimum age for both men and women to qualify for a social pension seems appropriate. Doing so is important from a labor supply incentive viewpoint, although it would need to maintain consistency with urban pension policy. Such a benefit would be noncontributory and financed by national, provincial, municipal, and local resources.

A social pension approach would be broadly consistent with the design of the basic benefit provision under the rural pension pilot. As noted above, any social pension should be subjected to a pension test, which would adjust the amount paid to those 65 to 74 years of age by a proportion of benefits they receive either from the individual account or from an urban workers' pension. The adjustment factor could be set as high as 50 percent initially (to provide a strong incentive to contribute to the individual account), but it should be adjusted on the basis of actual experience. A stylized example is provided in figure 6.3, using a benefit level linked to rural individual minimum consumption and applying a 50 percent adjustment factor.

As with the basic benefit under the national pilot, the value of a social pension relative to the *dibao* threshold in different localities is an important design parameter. In this regard, the practice of most current rural pension pilot schemes seems appropriate (that is, setting the social

Figure 6.3   Stylized Example of Rural Pension Benefit Levels and Composition under Proposed Scheme

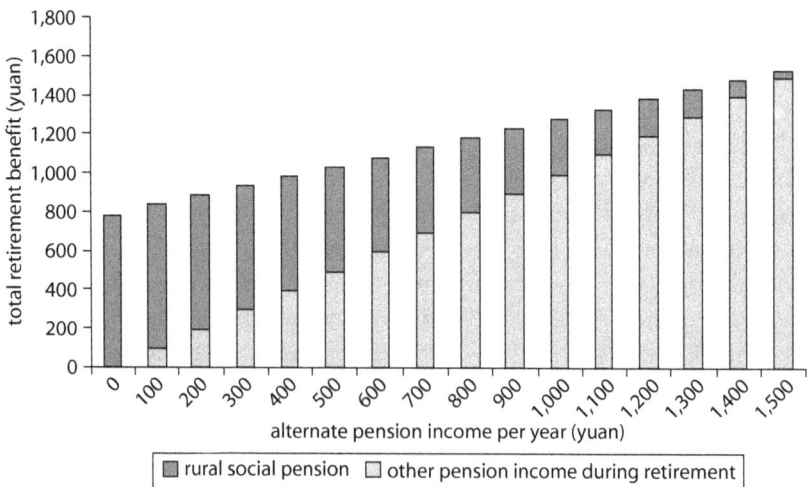

Source: World Bank forthcoming.
Note: Assumes social pension benefit of 788 yuan per year minus the Ravallion-Chen rural consumption poverty level increased by the CPI from 2003 to 2009. In this example, social pension benefit is reduced by 50 percent of alternative pension income.

pension at a level above the *dibao* per capita threshold). This practice is important for incentive reasons, but—for fiscal reasons—the level should not be substantially higher. If a social pension were set too high, the incentive to contribute to the individual account would be weaker; if it is set too low, its poverty alleviation objective may be undermined. Under the rural pension pilot, the central government has set the minimum flat benefit at RMB 55 monthly while allowing provision of additional funds from subnational sources. This minimum flat benefit compares with a national average rural *dibao* threshold of RMB 82 in 2008, with a range from a minimum of RMB 26 to RMB 267 (or 11 to 41 percent of the national rural average wage). The *dibao* threshold rates suggest that closer attention needs to be paid to the relative level of the social pension floor to align protections and incentives appropriately. Finally, pensions from current pilot rural pension schemes and any possible future social pension should not affect the receipt of the allowance for following family planning policies. However, some Chinese researchers have proposed integrating the programs by using the family planning subsidy as an additional subsidy toward individual pension contributions (Mi and Yang 2008; C. Yang 2007; Y. Yang 2007).

Indicative cost estimates suggest that a social pension set around the urban income poverty line would be about 0.11 percent of 2010 GDP, rising to 0.31 percent of GDP by 2040 (see figure 6.4).[10] A social pension set around the rural poverty consumption line would be about 0.13 percent of 2010 GDP, declining to about 0.12 percent of GDP by 2040. These estimates would vary substantially with the benefit level, the growth in the benefit level, the level of urbanization, and the observed benefit reductions arising from the pension test. The upward trend in cost projections reflects population aging and urbanization. By comparison, if the social pension were set at about 28 percent of the urban average wage (the OECD average), the cost would be 0.75 percent of GDP in 2010 and would rise to 2.10 percent of GDP by 2040.[11] Although the higher figure is probably more than China may wish to allocate to such a benefit, the experience of several OECD countries noted below suggests that a benefit level somewhere between the lower bound and the OECD average could be affordable.

Countries with all levels of income have widespread experience with noncontributory social pensions. The experience with reducing old-age poverty is generally positive, although issues of fiscal sustainability have arisen in lower-income settings. However, social pensions are proving to be an increasingly popular method for bridging the old-age coverage gap in pension systems.[12]

Figure 6.4   Indicative Cost Projections for Urban and Rural Social Pensions

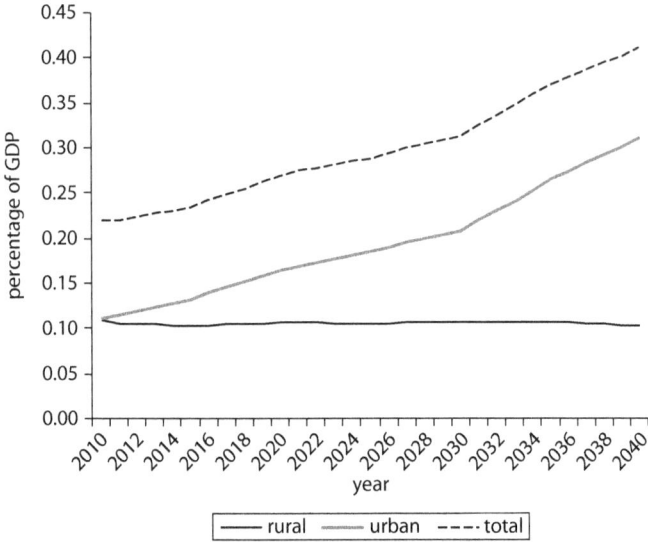

Source: World Bank staff estimates.
Note: Assumes (a) median variant urbanization 2010–40; (b) total fertility rate of 1.8; and (c) the age distribution for the population over age 60 is the same as for the total population. The rural reduction from the pension test and transition introduction is 5 percent in 2011, rising by 3 percent each year to a maximum of 50 percent. The urban reduction from the pension test is 40 percent in 2010, rising by 1 percent each year to a maximum of 60 percent. The benefit level is assumed to grow at the rate of GDP.

OECD countries have different approaches to social pensions (see table 6.1).[13] Although about half the countries rely on a single approach to social pensions, the remainder rely on combinations of three basic approaches:

- The *basic pension*, often called a "demogrant," is a flat benefit for the elderly awarded independently of income. Countries with basic pensions usually have some qualifying provisions, such as residency or contribution tests.
- A *resource-tested social pension* is provided either through a separate program for the elderly or as part of a general social assistance scheme. Eligibility is subject to some form of means testing, which can include income or income plus assets.
- The *minimum pension* is similar to a resource-tested pension in that it targets older people with lower incomes. The key difference is that only income from pension schemes is considered when calculating entitlement to a minimum pension. Consequently, someone with substantial

Table 6.1   Social Pensions in OECD Countries

Country	Resource tested	Basic	Minimum	Country	Resource tested	Basic	Minimum
Australia	X			Korea, Rep.	X		
Austria	X			Luxembourg	X		X
Belgium	X		X	Mexico	X		X
Canada	X	X		Netherlands	X		
Czech Republic		X	X	New Zealand	X		
Denmark	X	X		Norway	X		X
Finland			X	Poland			X
France	X		X	Portugal	X		X
Germany	X			Slovak Republic			X
Greece	X		X	Spain	X		X
Hungary			X	Sweden			X
Iceland	X	X		Switzerland	X		X
Ireland	X	X		Turkey	X		X
Italy	X			United Kingdom	X	X	X
Japan		X		United States	X		

Source: OECD 2007.

income from nonpension sources can still qualify. In countries where a contribution history is required to qualify for social pensions, periods of unemployment and disability are often counted toward the qualifying period. As a result, in practice, most people qualify.

Among OECD countries, the replacement rate from the social pension ranges from 20 to 40 percent of average economywide earnings, with a cross-country average of just under 30 percent (see figure 6.5). In Japan, for example, the rate is as low as 16 percent, whereas in Portugal it is well over 40 percent. Comparisons are complicated by the availability of general social assistance programs for the elderly. Over the past decade, a number of OECD countries have significantly reformed their social pension programs although no clear directional trend exists. Some countries (such as France, Ireland, the Republic of Korea, and Mexico) have introduced (or increased the basis for) minimum pensions. Others (such as Germany, Japan, and New Zealand) have cut earnings-related pensions with little effect on social pensions. Still others (such as Italy and several eastern European countries) have abolished minimum pensions altogether.[14]

As table 6.2 shows, the most significant difference in design is whether noncontributory social pensions are universal, means tested, or categorical

Figure 6.5   Value of Social Pensions as a Percentage of Average Earnings in OECD Countries

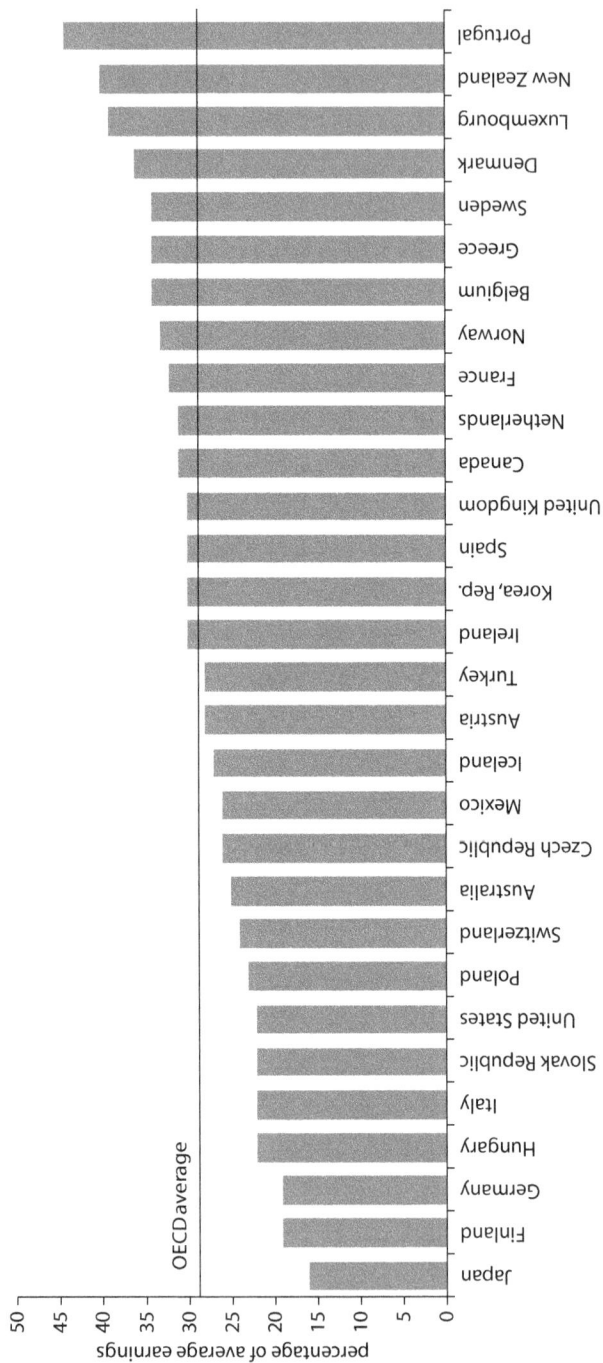

percentage of average earnings

OECD average

Portugal
New Zealand
Luxembourg
Denmark
Sweden
Greece
Belgium
Norway
France
Netherlands
Canada
United Kingdom
Spain
Korea, Rep.
Ireland
Turkey
Austria
Iceland
Mexico
Czech Republic
Australia
Switzerland
Poland
United States
Slovak Republic
Italy
Hungary
Germany
Finland
Japan

50 45 40 35 30 25 20 15 10 5 0

Source: OECD 2007.

128

Table 6.2 Inventory of Noncontributory Pension Programs in Developing Countries

Country	Date of recent law	Type of program	Administration	Eligibility age
Argentina	1993	Means test	Ministry of Social Development	70
Bangladesh	1998	Means test	Ministry of Social Welfare	57
Bolivia	1993	Universal but cohort restricted	Ministry of Economic Development	65
Botswana	1996	Universal	Department of Labor and Social Security	65
Brazil	(1974)	Means test	National Social Security Institute (INSS)	67
(Social Assistance [RMV]/	1993	Means test, basic		60 for men,
BPC Rural Pension)	1992	contributory record		55 for women
Chile	1980 and 1981	Means test	Ministry of Development and Planning	70
Costa Rica	1995	Means test	Costa Rican Social Insurance Fund	65
India	1995	Means test	Ministry of Labor	65
Mauritius	1976	Universal	Ministry of Social Security and Solidarity	60
Namibia	1990	Universal	Government Pension Fund (GIPF)	60
Nepal	1995–6	Universal	Ministry of Local Development	75
Samoa	1990	Universal	Labor Department and Accident Compensation Board	65
South Africa	1992 (amended in 1997)	Means test	National and Provincial Departments of Social Development	65 for men, 60 for women
Sri Lanka	1939	Means test	Provincial Department of Social Services	
Uruguay	1995	Means test	Ministry of Labor and Social Security and Social Welfare Fund	70

Source: World Bank staff estimates.

in coverage. No definitive pattern by level of income emerges in this respect. The broad distinction is sometimes drawn between social pension systems that are core elements of old-age security and those that are supplementary (either to contributory systems or to informal support systems). This distinction can be determined by comparing the combination of coverage rates among the elderly and benefit levels relative to country income, as figure 6.6 shows for selected developing countries.

With respect to the age of eligibility, experience also differs, but 65 to 70 is most common (see table 6.2). The financing source for social pensions also varies across countries, although general revenues are most common. Brazil, in contrast, funds its social pension scheme from a 2 percent contribution from rural employers.

Figure 6.6   Ratio of Social Pension to per Capita Income Multiplied by Ratio of Number of Recipients to Number of Elderly

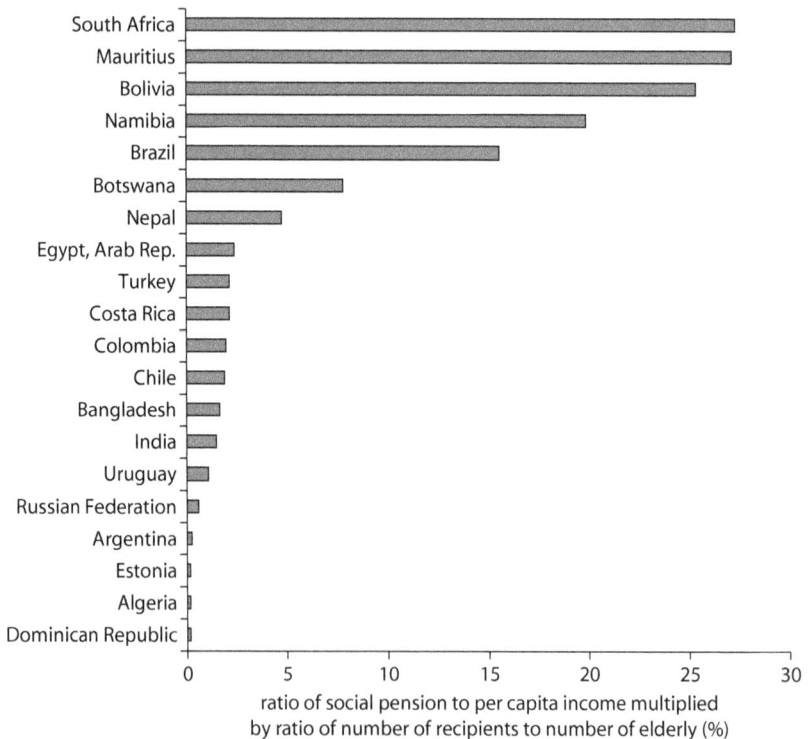

ratio of social pension to per capita income multiplied by ratio of number of recipients to number of elderly (%)

Source: Palacios and Robalino 2009.

The effect of social pension schemes in developing countries is generally positive in alleviating old-age poverty, although evidence is limited. Core schemes (found in Bolivia, Botswana, Brazil, Mauritius, Namibia, and South Africa) have been shown to reduce old-age poverty significantly, whereas supplementary schemes have varied more widely in their targeting and their outcomes in poverty reduction.[15] Evidence for other effects from social pension schemes is even more limited, coming primarily from Bolivia, Brazil, and South Africa. The effects seem to be mixed. Positive effects may include permanent increases in income from the investment of transfers, better health indicators, and higher school enrollment rates for children from pensioner households. Negative effects may include a reduction in labor supply on the part of other household members. The evidence is mixed on the reduction of family support to the elderly.

Countries have also managed the interaction between social pension schemes and defined contribution schemes in different ways. Chile serves as an interesting example. In its 2008 reform, Chile introduced a new *solidarity pension* with the twofold objectives of (a) achieving universal pension coverage and (b) reducing old-age poverty more effectively. The solidarity pension also aims to better integrate the country's contributory system and the noncontributory system. The solidarity pension targets men and women over 65 (who are among the poorest 60 percent of the population) and is subject to a national residence requirement. A universal basic pension was established for people with no individual account accumulations. Those with a contribution history and individual account accumulations, however, are eligible to have their funded pension benefit augmented subject to a ceiling on the combined amount. As a result, the supplement (known as the "solidarity contribution") shrinks for individuals with higher account balances. The withdrawal of the solidarity pension is designed to retain incentives to sustain higher contributions to the funded portion of the scheme. People with higher income levels are permitted to supplement their individual account balances with voluntary contributions. Figure 6.7 illustrates the scheme in graphical form. From a design viewpoint, the system strikes a useful balance between creating incentives to contribute and providing basic old-age protection for those with low or no contribution history (although concerns have been raised with respect to its projected fiscal cost).

Figure 6.7   Chile's System of Solidarity Pensions, Introduced in 2008

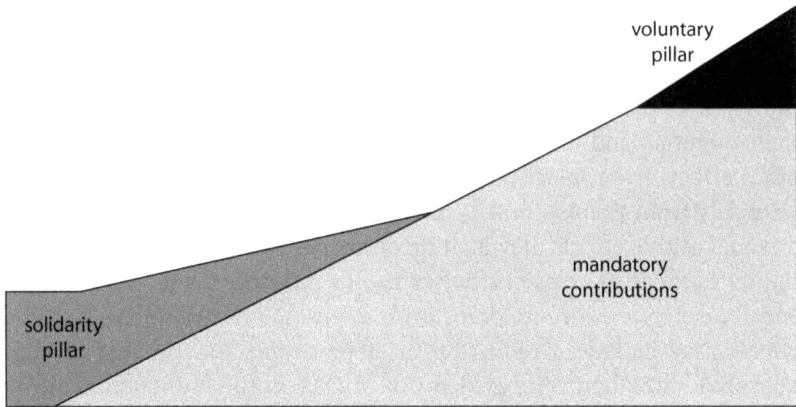

Source: Fajnzylber, PowerPoint slide, 2008.

The Interaction between Individual Accounts and the Social Pension and the Transitional Generation

A key policy decision relates to whether individual accounts and the basic benefit (or social pension) should be combined over time as the contributory system matures. The two broad options are (a) to retain a basic benefit (or social pension) for people over a certain age to provide an income floor that is supplemented by benefits from individual accounts (if chosen, a number of questions must be addressed regarding the interaction between the basic benefit level and eligibility criteria and the contributory pension, as was illustrated in the case of Chile) or (b) to gradually phase out the basic benefit (or social pension) as the contributory system matures, addressing elderly poverty through the regular social assistance program (perhaps, as is the case in a number of urban areas already, with an elderly supplement on the *dibao* threshold or benefit level). This book recommends retaining the basic benefit (or social pension) even in the longer run.

In either case, a targeted benefit level from the combination of the basic benefit (or social pension) and individual accounts must be established, ideally falling between the poverty line and the average wage. The specific target should depend on the fiscal envelope and social policy decisions relating to work incentives as people age. The target should be indexed over time against prices or per capita incomes (or some combination of the two). This book recommends basing indexation policies on some mixture of prices and wages, with prices the major factor to meet poverty-alleviation objectives.

Policy makers must decide how to handle those approaching retirement who will have insufficient time to contribute enough to their accounts to earn a reasonable pension. Special treatment is needed to manage this transition. The issue has been dealt with in a variety of ways under previous rural pension pilots in China, and a number of schemes have special treatment for people older than 45. Baoji, for example, allowed those over 45 to receive a full pension if they contributed until they reach 60; those over 60 were also entitled, subject to "family binding." This approach is the same as that adopted in the rural pension pilot. Some schemes have provisions for the lump-sum payment of contributions by those without a full contribution history; in some cases, at the point of retirement (for example, Beijing and Zhuhai) and in others during the accumulation phase. Other schemes have older cohorts continue to make contributions for up to five years after reaching the normal retirement age.

One option for dealing with the transitional generation (defined, for example, as people over 50 in the year they start contributing) is to notionally credit their accounts with full individual and matched contributions for all the years in which they did not contribute, assuming a standard age of entry into the scheme of somewhere between 20 and 25.

Moving from Rural Pensions to a Residents' Pension?

Apart from the issues discussed above, a further consideration for a pension system for rural populations is the future integration of urban and rural pension systems and the issue of portability. Although integration is unlikely in the foreseeable future, implying full equalization of benefits between rural and urban areas (just as the current urban system does not provide the same benefits everywhere), a common design framework would be useful to facilitate portability between systems. Such a framework can already be seen in several areas, where integrated rural and urban residents' pension schemes are in place (for example, Zhongshan in Guangdong Province). In recent years, rural migrant workers have tended to stay longer in their destination location, with about two-thirds of migrant workers remaining resident for three or more years. This practice reflects the long-term trend in the labor market toward greater urbanization. In such cases, the need to move workers' pension accumulations and entitlements with them—or "totalize" their benefits between different locations so they can enjoy them from different locations at retirement—will become increasingly important. These bigger-picture integration issues will quickly become key concerns for the evolving rural pension system as it consolidates during the 12th Five-Year Plan period.

Conclusion

The issues outlined in this chapter suggest that some adaptations of the national rural pension pilot have the potential to strengthen the system over time. They are offered as options the government could consider as it expands the current schemes for rural and urban workers. In any case, the issues discussed address only the general framework and would need elaboration to become operational. However, they may over time help strike a reasonable balance among concerns for elderly welfare, fiscal demands, and labor market effects. The current rural pension pilot is clearly a major step in the right direction and provides a solid foundation from which to think about evolution of the rural pension system over the coming decade and later. This book has shown a seemingly compelling rationale for public intervention in the welfare of the elderly who are not already covered by urban pension systems, and the new rural pension pilot demonstrates the government's commitment to achieving its goal of universal social security coverage this decade.

Notes

1. This chapter is an adapted and shortened form of the annex on rural pensions in *China: A Vision for Pension Policy Reform Options* (World Bank forthcoming). That paper covers all elements of the Chinese pension system in a more comprehensive manner.

2. For a comprehensive discussion of recent experiences with "closing the coverage gap" through the extension of pension systems to rural and informal sector populations, see Holzmann, Robalino, and Takayama (2009) and Palacios and Robalino (2009) on the framework for matching defined contribution schemes.

3. See (a) Lin (2006) for European, Commonwealth of Independent States, and low-income countries; (b) Gong (2006) for Japan; (c) Su (2007) for the Republic of Korea; and (d) Leisering, Sen, and Hussain (2002) and Zheng (2007) for a general discussion of the subsidy approach.

4. Localized examples of collectives in urban areas have solid revenue bases from the rental of collective land to factories or for other users that may be able to provide significant matching, whereas rural collectives may not.

5. See Zheng (2007) regarding a reserve fund proposal. See Lü (2005) for proposals for higher-return portfolio options.

6. Examples of contracting arrangements in other countries offer the benefits of competition among asset managers while limiting the number of asset managers to ensure a critical mass of funds and generate economies of scale in fund management (for example, India's new pension scheme and a number of funded pillar schemes in Central Asia, Europe, and Latin America). However, most of these countries have more developed regulatory and accountability frameworks than China does at present (see Rajkumar and Dorfnum, 2011).

7. See Holzmann and Palmer (2006) for a comprehensive review of notional defined contributions.

8. See http://www.cnr.cn/china/gdgg/201009/t20100907_507012375.html, accessed October 12, 2011.

9. This section draws on Palacios and Robalino (2009).

10. These figures assume a benefit level of 1,200 yuan per year (about 4.1 percent of the projected urban average wage) beginning in 2010.

11. For comparison purposes, the reduction resulting from the application of the pension test is assumed to be the same in the two scenarios. Realistically, the cost reduction in the application of the pension test should be greater in the second of the two scenarios because the benefit before the reduction is far higher.

12. See Palacios and Sluchynskyy (2006). See also Asher for middle-income countries and Barrientos for lower-income countries, both cited in Holzmann, Robalino, and Takayama (2009).

13. See Pearson and Whitehouse (2009) for a discussion of social pensions in high-income countries.

14. See Pearson and Whitehouse (2009) for details on the effect of these pension reforms on net replacement rates by earning level.

15. See Kakwani and Subbarao (2005) on African schemes, Barrientos (2009) on four developing countries, and Palacios and Sluchynsky (2006) for an international overview.

References

Barrientos, Armando. 2009. "Social Pensions in Low-Income Countries." In *Closing the Coverage Gap: The Role of Social Pensions and Other Retirement Income Transfers*, ed. Robert Holzmann, David Robalino, and Noriyuki Takayama, 73–84. Washington, DC: World Bank.

Benjamin, Daniel J. 2003. "Does 401(k) Eligibility Increase Saving?: Evidence from Propensity Score Subclassification." *Journal of Public Economics* 87 (5–6): 1259–90.

Engen, Eric M., and William G. Gale. 2000. "The Effects of 401(k) Plans on Household Wealth: Differences across Earnings Groups." NBER Working Paper 8032, National Bureau of Economic Research, Cambridge, MA.

Gong, Xiaoxia. 2006. "Rural Pension System and Its Lessons in Developed Countries." [In Chinese.] *Journal of Central Finance University* 6.

Holzmann, Robert, and Edward Palmer, eds. 2006. *Pension Reform: Issues and Prospects for Non-Financial Defined Contribution (NDCs) Schemes.* Washington, DC: World Bank.

Holzmann, Robert, David Robalino, and Noriuki Takayama, eds. 2009. *Closing the Coverage Gap: Role of Social Pensions and Other Retirement Income Transfers.* Washington, DC: World Bank.

Kakwani, Nanak, and Kalanidhi Subbarao. 2005. "Aging and Poverty in Africa and the Role of Social Pensions." Social Protection Discussion Paper 521, World Bank, Washington, DC.

Leisering, Lutz, Gong Sen, and Athar Hussain. 2002. *People's Republic of China: Old-Age Pensions for the Rural Areas: From Land Reform to Globalization.* Manila, Philippines: Asian Development Bank.

Lin, Yi. 2006. *Research on International Comparison of Rural Social Security and Its Lessons.* [In Chinese.] Beijing: China Labor and Social Security Publishing House.

Lü, Jiming. 2005. "Current Situation of Rural Social Security and Analysis of Its Development Path." [In Chinese.] *Journal of Ningxia Communist School* 6.

Mi, Hong, and Cuiying Yang. 2008. *Basic Theoretic Framework Research on Rural Pension System.* [In Chinese.] Guang Ming Publishing House, Shanghai.

OECD (Organisation for Economic Co-operation and Development). 2007. *Pensions at a Glance.* Paris: OECD.

Palacios, Robert, and David Robalino. 2009. "Matching Defined Contributions: A Way to Increase Pension Coverage." In *Closing the Coverage Gap: The Role of Social Pensions and Other Retirement Income Transfers,* ed. Robert Holzmann, David Robalino, and Noriyuki Takayama, 187–202. Washington, DC: World Bank.

Palacios, Robert, and Oleksiy Sluchynsky. 2006. "Social Pensions Part I: Their Role in the Overall Pension System." Social Protection Discussion Paper 36237, World Bank, Washington, DC.

Pearson, Mark, and Edward Whitehouse. 2009. "Social Pensions in High-Income Countries." In *Closing the Coverage Gap: The Role of Social Pensions and Other Retirement Income Transfers,* ed. Robert Holzmann, David Robalino, and Noriyuki Takayama, 99–110. Washington, DC: World Bank.

Rajkumar, Sudhir and Mark Dorfnum (2011). Governance and Investment of Public Pension Assets: Practitioners' perspectives, World Bank, Washington, DC.

Ravallion, Martin, and Shaohua Chen. 2007. "China's (Uneven) Progress against Poverty." *Journal of Development Economics* 82 (1): 1–42.

Su, Baozhong. 2007. "Rural Pension Systems of Western Developed Countries and Its Lessons." [In Chinese.] *Current Economy* 12.

World Bank. Forthcoming. *China: A Vision for Pension Policy Reform Options.* Washington, DC: World Bank.

Wu, Yuning. 2009. "Literature Review of China Rural Pension System." Background paper prepared for World Bank East Asia Social Protection Unit, Beijing.

Yang, Cuiying. 2007. *Nong cun ji ben yang lao bao xian zhi du li lun yu zheng ce yan jiu.* [Studies on rural social pension insurance system in China: Practice, theory, and policy]. Hangzhou: Zhejiang da xue chu ban she.

Yang, Jianiguo. 2007. "Innovation and Selection of Financing Sources of Rural Social Security." Developing Research 2007 (2).

Yoo, Kwang-Yeol, and Alain de Serres. 2004. "Tax Treatment of Private Pension Savings in OECD Countries and the Net Tax Cost per Unit of Contribution to Tax-Favoured Schemes." OECD Economics Department Working Papers 406, OECD Publishing, Paris.

Zheng, Wei. 2007. "Reflection on the Dilemma of China Rural Pension System." [In Chinese.] *Insurance Research* 11.

Data Sources for Analysis of Rural Elderly Welfare

Data source	Years	Topics	Organizations
China Health and Nutrition Survey (CHNS)	1991 1993 1997 2002 2004 2006	This survey was designed to examine the effects of health, nutrition, and family planning policies and programs implemented by national and local governments and to see how the socioeconomic transformation of Chinese society affects the health and nutritional status of its population.	Carolina Population Center at the University of North Carolina, Chapel Hill, http://www .cpc.unc.edu/projects/china, and the National Institute of Nutrition and Food Safety at the Chinese Center for Disease Control and Prevention
Rural Household Survey; Follow-up survey conducted in 2004	Annual surveys 1995–2006	This survey was designed to examine the developmental status of the rural economy by collecting longitudinal household information on household demography, agricultural production, nonagricultural employment, income, and expenditures. This book uses two samples—a four-province sample from 1995 to 2003 plus the follow-up survey on labor, demography, and governance conducted in 2004—to examine private transfers and changing labor supply patterns. A more recent sample (2003–06) from eight provinces was used in the analysis of saving decisions.	Research Center for Rural Economy, Ministry of Agriculture
Population Census	1982 1990 2000	The population census collected information on all individuals who lived in rural and urban China at the surveyed time. It contains information on demographic characteristics, employment, and housing.	National Bureau of Statistics

One Percent Population Sample Data	2005	This sample is similar to the population census but only draws on 1 percent of total population.	National Bureau of Statistics
China Urban and Rural Elderly Survey (CURES)	2006	This survey was designed to collect information on income and expenditure, health, social security, living arrangement, and status of urban and rural elderly.	China Research Center on Aging, Ministry of Civil Affairs
China Population Statistical Yearbook	1991–2006	It contains information on population and employment in rural and urban areas.	National Bureau of Statistics
China Population and Employment Statistical Yearbook	2007 2008 2009	It contains information on population and employment in rural and urban areas.	National Bureau of Statistics
Labor and Social Security Yearbook	2001–08	It contains information on social security.	Ministry of Human Resources and Social Security
World Population Prospects: 2008 Revision	2008	It is a worldwide population projection data source.	Population Division of the Department of Economic and Social Affairs of the UN Secretariat

Index

www.ingramcontent.com/pod-product-compliance
Lightning Source LLC
Chambersburg PA
CBHW070920270326
41927CB00011B/2660